OVERTIME

OVERTIME

Why We Need a Shorter Working Week

WILL STRONGE and KYLE LEWIS

VERSO

London • New York

First published by Verso 2021
© Will Stronge and Kyle Lewis 2021

1 3 5 7 9 10 8 6 4 2

Verso
UK: 6 Meard Street, London W1F 0EG
US: 20 Jay Street, Suite 1010, Brooklyn, NY 11201
versobooks.com

Verso is the imprint of New Left Books

ISBN-13: 978-1-78873-868-2
ISBN-13: 978-1-78873-869-9 (UK EBK)
ISBN-13: 978-1-78873-870-5 (US EBK)

British Library Cataloguing in Publication Data
A catalogue record for this book is available from the British Library

Library of Congress Cataloging-in-Publication Data
Library of Congress Control Number: 2021937562

Typeset in Sabon by Biblichor Ltd, Edinburgh
Printed and bound by CPI Group (UK) Ltd, Croydon CR0 4YY

Contents

Acknowledgements

We would like to acknowledge all of the staff and affiliates that have passed through Autonomy over the past three years: it is because of that organisation that this book has come about. We'd also like to say thank you to John Merrick for his patience and contributions as an editor.

INTRODUCTION: A FIGHT AS OLD AS CAPITALISM ITSELF

The Monday to Friday working week that many of us see as normal or natural is in fact a social and historical achievement, and one that is still unevenly distributed – with workers in many parts of the world labouring round the clock, seven days a week, for almost nothing. The free time that we enjoy in much of the Global North is the result of victories achieved by workers in the nineteenth and twentieth centuries. It was the Australian stonemasons that first won the eight-hour day in 1856.[1] While building an ever expanding Melbourne, James Stephens and his colleagues had had enough of the gruelling ten-hour workdays, and so at a meeting of fellow construction workers, they concluded that 'the time has arrived when the system of eight hours should be introduced into the building trades.'[2] This demand took more than mere words however. On 21 April, Stephens and colleagues walked off the job at Melbourne University in order to march to the Belvedere Hotel, picking up other construction workers on the way to join their endeavour. Fittingly, their show of strength ended with a banquet at the hotel itself – where the manual labourers could revel in their collective stand. Following months of talks with their employers, their demand was met – as reported in the local *Herald*:

> [The masons] have succeeded, at least in all the building trades in enforcing [the eight-hour day] without effort. The employers have found it necessary . . . to give in, and without struggle; agreeing, we believe, to pay the same amount of wages as formerly for ten hours' labour.[3]

The celebration of this historic victory for workers – known initially as the '8 Hours Procession' – was commemerated for ninety-five years and ultimately became synchronised with international 'Labour Day' celebrations.

The stonemasons' example – alongside many other struggles over working time throughout history – can teach us at least two things: first, that our freedom from the hardships of work is rarely, if ever, given to us; it must be demanded and fought for. Second, it suggests that working time reduction is an aspiration of working people in whatever form of employment, in whatever epoch of capitalism. It was clear to those stoneworkers then – as it is clear to us now – that being able to relax, spend time with loved ones, pursue self-directed activity and have freedom from a boss are all essential parts of what it means to be human. Time is life after all.

Working time is still the issue
Yet this struggle over the time we spend at work is not one that has been consigned to the past. Once again, the fight for a shorter working week is back on the political agenda. Politicians across the Global North have in recent years reignited the political debate, not least Alexandria Ocasio-Cortez in the US, Sanna Marin in Finland, former Shadow Chancellor John McDonnell in the UK and Jacinda Ardern in New Zealand.[4] Trade unions such as IG Metall in Germany, the Communication Workers Union in the UK, and Forsa in Ireland were all in the middle of campaigns for hours reductions before the Covid pandemic caused mass unemployment. And even more trade unions have joined the chorus since. Across the world, companies large and small are adopting shorter working weeks – with no reduction in pay – for their staff: from two thousand Microsoft employees in Japan,[5] to a small board games company in London.[6] The shorter working week is no longer a

fringe campaign; instead, it is a central aspect of the renewal of socialist politics that has taken place in the past decade.

In some sense, the newfound public attention on working time is unsurprising: it is, after all, a structuring factor in all of our lives. Everyone in society has to reckon, in some way or another, with how long they work each week – whether they have a job, are self-employed or work unpaid in the domestic sphere; whether they work too many hours, can't get enough hours or can't get a job at all. Work defines and determines all of our lives, from an early age right up until our final years.

We should note that in this book we'll be talking mainly about working time in terms of employment, and largely in the context of the Global North. Of course, this doesn't mean that other forms of work, or work in the Global South, are unimportant to the discussion – far from it. Indeed, in the following chapters we integrate discussions of unwaged work and 'shadow work' into our argument at various points, and we point to those theoretical and empirical resources for understanding global supply chains, which offer much greater analyses of these phenomena than we can here. Other forms of commodification of human activity – such as slavery – have long powered capitalist economies alongside wage labour, both physically, sometimes in the very same workplace, but also contemporaneously, across different continents, within the same value chain.[7] We also shouldn't forget or ignore the fact that slavery still exists around the world to this day.[8]

The crisis of work today

The renewed impetus that campaigns for a shorter working week are currently experiencing has come about in the context of a degraded labour market. If 'hard work' at your job ever guaranteed an improvement in your situation, this is far from assured now. Over the past few decades, the share of national income going to wages and salaries has declined, while the share going to capital has expanded, meaning that simply owning assets such as shares or housing is a more expedient route to economic success; 'earning' a living is an anachronistic term.

Research has shown that over time and across the globe, a higher capital share (and lower labour share) is linked with higher inequality in terms of the distribution of personal incomes.[9] As it stands in the UK, around 12 per cent of the population own 50 per cent of private wealth.[10] Unsurprisingly, some are calling this new economy 'rentier capitalism', where those who inherit wealth or simply own assets thrive and where 'work does not pay' for the many.[11]

Workers are getting a raw deal in more subtle ways too. They put in large amounts of unpaid overtime;[12] are commuting for longer than they were even just ten years ago;[13] are earning less in real terms than they have for over a decade;[14] and are suffering remarkable levels of in-work poverty.[15] The number of precarious jobs – those that cannot guarantee a secure livelihood – has risen sharply this century, with over 1 million zero-hours contracts deployed in 2017 and bogus 'self-employment' taking basic rights away from workers.[16] There are indications that the Covid-19 pandemic will only exacerbate this increase in 'non-standard' work. Deliveroo and Amazon – both notoriously poor employers – have announced the creation of thousands of new jobs, partly as a consequence of high street retailers and food outlets closing due to lockdown.[17] As well as a scarcity of decent work for some, there is an abundance of work-driven burnout for many others. According to statistics from the British government, over half of all sick absences in the UK are due to work-related stress, anxiety or depression, with workload being the number one reason given for these afflictions.[18]

Traditionally, it has been the role of organised labour to prevent the degradation of labour and push for a better world of work. It is no accident that during the period when we saw significant reduction in working time – the interwar years in both the UK and US – trade union membership was high, and their remits were radical. During the 1980s, there was a sustained political project across much of the Global North to smash the collective power of workers. Following this, the space in which workers could have a say in how the labour market is run, and in whose interest, has been significantly squeezed. Consecutive, regressive labour legislation in the UK such as the Employment Act (1980) and the Trade Union Act (1984), as well as the present failure to clamp down on the bogus self-employment enacted by platforms such as Uber and Deliveroo, have contributed to the neutering of progressive labour market reform, and have meant that once-traditional trade union demands for such working time reduction have become increasingly remote from the mainstream agenda.

It has been estimated that the UK is now the country with the second lowest level of collective bargaining coverage in Europe.[19] Today, coverage could perhaps be as low as 20 per cent, in comparison to over 70 per cent in the 1960s and 1970s.[20] This decline has been facilitated in large part by hostile policy: even Tony Blair once remarked that British law on trade unions is the 'most restrictive in the Western World'.[21]

In short, modern work – particularly, but not exclusively, in the US and UK – has reached new lows in terms of working conditions, the types of jobs available and the decision-making power that working people have in the workplace. Perhaps in this sense, we are again closer to Friedrich Engels's 1845 *The Conditions of the Working Class in England,* a devastating investigation of the extreme poverty and social deprivation endured by the working class in Victorian England, a work that was tragically mirrored in 2018 by a UN report examining extreme poverty and human rights in the UK. The report's author, Professor Philip Alston, articulated the way in which the labour market, and social security system that underpins it, have resulted in extreme levels of poverty and social deprivation:

14 million people, a fifth of the population, live in poverty. Four million of these are more than 50 per cent below the poverty line, and 1.5 million are destitute, unable to afford basic essentials. The widely respected Institute for Fiscal Studies predicts a 7 per cent rise in child poverty between 2015 and 2022, and various sources predict child poverty rates of as high as 40 per cent. For almost one in every two children to be poor in twenty-first century Britain is not just a disgrace, but a social calamity and an economic disaster, all rolled into one.[22]

Many of the harrowing stories outlined in Engel's description of life in Victorian Britain are replicated in Alston's accounts of minimum wage work and welfare 'support', epitomised by the roll-out of the benefit payment Universal Credit. Rather than alleviating poverty and providing freedom and security to its citizens, work in twenty-first century Britain is defined by insecure contracts, punitive surveillance and a wage that doesn't meet the basic needs of life:

> Low wages, insecure jobs, and zero-hour contracts mean that even at record unemployment there are still 14 million people in poverty . . . One pastor said 'The majority of people using our food bank are in work . . . Nurses and teachers are accessing food banks.'[23]

In circumstances like this, overwork becomes a necessary condition for survival, with those in the UK working the third highest number of hours in Europe.[24] Much of our devotion to work hinges on a certain cultural norm, and a restricted political imagination, whereby work is regarded as not only being a good in and of itself but also a condition of individual health and social well-being. David Frayne calls this the 'employment dogma', which often makes a link between employment and good health being somehow natural or innate to human flourishing.[25] What's clear from history, however, is that without significant collective organising and political regulation, *the labour market fails in delivering a robust mechanism for economic security and freedom to all.*

We must therefore recognise that mere employment cannot be considered a sufficient condition for providing individual health and economic security alone. Work's ability to aid human flourishing should only be considered sufficient if it can provide the social conditions that would allow all humans to cooperate, structure their time, achieve a sense of dignity and obtain the necessary material means to live in a safe and secure environment.

A 'multi-dividend' policy

In advocating for a shorter working week, Rutger Bregman poses the following provocation: 'What does working less actually solve? Perhaps it's better to turn this question around and ask: Is there anything that working less does not solve?'[26] Across our chapters, we want to stress how shortening the working week would have multiple beneficial effects on our societies.

A shorter working week is not just an intervention on work alone, it is also a feminist issue – helping to equalise the distribution of both paid and unpaid, usually feminised, labour in the household – as well as a green policy: by working less we can provide one pillar for the rapid decarbonisation of our economy, and it could have profound effects on many other areas as well.

The examples of the stonemasons and the garment factory workers of the nineteenth and early twentieth centuries show us that struggles over working time are common to capitalism; they also show us that victories in reducing working time can have long-lasting effects that we now take for granted. The same struggle for freedom now lies before the workers of the twenty-first century: the admin assistants, the call centre workers, the teachers, the care workers, the warehouse operatives and those still in manufacturing.

It has been over eighty years since President Roosevelt's New Deal put hours caps into legislation in the US and over seventy since the UK established the forty-hour work week as the new standard. Since then, the world has changed rapidly. New technologies and business strategies have moulded our workplaces and lives, economic ideologies have replaced one another in turn, and yet our working hours have remained largely the same or have even increased.

This long delay of progress tells us that working time reduction does not come about naturally, made possible by the sorcery of automation or on the shoulders of the giants of industry. Instead, working time is, and always has been, a political matter regarding the distribution of wealth and power in society. Once our ways of working have become denaturalised – a project that this book intends to contribute to – and we have greater decision-making capacity over the *purpose* of our economies, then the question of *how we work* – and *how long for* – confronts us.

Should we accept the continued dominance of work in our lives? Can we imagine different and more equal ways of working for ourselves? Crucially, how do we get there? The following chapters argue that it's time we take the next step in prioritising freedom over work, our lives over our jobs, and shorten the working week once again.

1 – LIVING IN THE WORK-OBSESSED SOCIETY

The weary sigh of the over-driven slave, pitilessly exploited and regarded as an animated tool or beast of burden: the medieval serf fast bound to the soil, and life-long prisoner on his lord's domain, subject to all the caprices of his lord's lust or anger: the modern wage-slave, with nothing but his labour to sell selling that, with his manhood as a wrapper, in the world's market-place for a mess of potage: these three phases of slavery, each in their turn inevitable and unavoidable, will have exhausted the possibilities of slavery, and mankind shall at last have leisure and inclination to really live as men, and not as the beasts which perish.[1]

In 1912, during one of the high points of struggle for the British labour movement, the Unofficial Reform Committee of the South Wales Miners issued a powerful manifesto outlining what the authors, including the miner and trade union leader Noah Ablett together with A. J. Cook, William Henry

Mainwaring and others, saw as the path for the future development of the mining industry. The manifesto speaks with a determination and a utopian hope that can still stir our own desires for a world beyond toil and drudgery even today. Yet, there is one striking aspect to it, one that may seem anachronistic. In its spirited mixture of Marxism and Syndicalism, it calls not merely for *better* jobs, but instead issues a demand for a future where we are no longer forced to work for a wage *at all*.

The fight for free time has accompanied capitalism ever since its emergence around four hundred years ago. But why? Why is time such an important terrain of conflict, negotiation and contestation? A large part of the answer lies in the way in which our economies function at the most basic level. We are no longer in Eric Hobsbawm's 'Age of Capital' from where the traditional images of gruelling work conditions – with their attendant long, grinding hours of labour – often stem. Yet time, and our lack of it, remains an important issue, even in a world of technological marvels and vast national wealth. Work's grip tightens around us: from school and its emphasis on getting qualifications for employment, to the power that your manager wields over you when you're on the job; from answering emails on the weekend, to the constant job applications and CV-building. Asking why so much of our time is taken up by employment – and what the nature of our working time is like on the job itself – helps us understand why workers of all kinds have struggled against the length of the working week throughout history.[2]

Time, freedom and work

Time is freedom. Or rather, time is a necessary foundation for freedom. Without the time available to us to actualise our potential, to exercise our minds and bodies, we simply cannot *do* the things we'd like, under our own volition. There are of course the day-to-day tasks we must carry out in order to survive – the reproductive functions of eating, sleeping and so on. But beyond the time of necessity, to paraphrase, lies the time of freedom, and this is ultimately the time that is most important to us.

Yet, within capitalism, time is also money. People are paid for quantities of their time in the form of a wage or salary, and within this paid time, as much output is expected of them as possible by an employer. Time, from this view, is another production cost in the drive for profitable business.

It is precisely this aspect of time, or the contrast between time as a foundation for human freedom on the one hand, and time as a measure of production and profit on the other, that Marx, one of capitalism's

most astute observers, saw as a reflection of the different sets of interests of those involved. From the
workers' perspective, employment is a means to the
wages necessary to meet one's (and perhaps one's
family's) needs. Beyond that, we might also expect
wages to provide the ability to pursue interests and
'live a life'. Our interest as an employee, then, is in
getting our wage; the cash with which to buy goods
necessary for life, as well as the commodities we want
for our leisure, for our socialising, and for what Marx
calls our 'intellectual needs'. The catch here, however,
is that in order to enjoy the life we have worked for, we
also need time, and it is precisely the time of life that
our bosses want to capture.

From the employer's perspective,[3] workers are
employed in order to perform a role in the productive
process: they produce for profit, and must be kept on
track to do so. This basic imperative frames how
employers see the company's work processes, its
investments, and the hours and pay of staff (now just
another element in production). All time is potential
production time within a capitalist economy; time can
and should always be turned into money if you want
to succeed as a business. According to Marx:

The worker [from the perspective of capital accu-
mulation] is nothing other than labour-power for

the duration of his whole life, and that therefore all his disposable time is by nature and by right labour-time, to be devoted to the self-valorisation of capital. Time for education, for intellectual development, for the fulfillment of social functions, for social intercourse, for the free play of the vital forces of his body and mind, even the rest time of Sunday – what foolishness![4]

Here we see these two demands running up against one another: those of the worker for more free time, away from work, and in contrast, the business pressure for longer hours, for squeezing more labour from their workers. This fight over time is inherent to employment, and is no mere remnant of the giant factories and warehouses of the industrial revolution, continuing to this day in various forms. We see this fight, this struggle, play out every day as we labour for a living. Who hasn't had a boss that checks our lunch breaks, who makes sure that we are all meeting our targets, that no one is 'underperforming', who watches anxiously as staff chat casually on the job, going about their work at their own speed? Equally, who hasn't scrolled through social media while at work, or taken five minutes extra for lunch, or gone for their fourth cup of tea that morning? These common experiences are evidently not demonstrations of evil or

immoral individuals – the 'bad boss' vs the 'slacker' –
but are expressions of the structural pressure to
control time, and the opposite desire not to be controlled by it that a profit-driven system brings. As
Marx puts it,

> It is evident that this does not depend on the will,
> either good or bad, or the individual capitalist.
> Under free competition, the immanent laws of
> capitalist production confront the individual capi-
> talist as a coercive force external to him.[5]

The 'immanent laws' of competition referred to here
index the constant pressure on firms to keep labour
costs low and outputs high. The time of work, or
rather the time that humans can be *put to work*, in
this scenario, is crucial to a business's calculations.

The labour-obsessed society

Working time is so important to the functioning
of capitalism that Marx devoted an entire chapter of
Capital to a discussion of the fight of workers to
decrease it during the nineteenth century in England.
Marx used contemporary reports of industrial
disputes to reflect on the nature of the employment
relationship, stressing that the length of the working
day is a variable quantity, one that is determined by

the different imperatives baked into the social relations at play. It is feasible, Marx provokes us to
imagine, for the working day to be only as long as it
takes to produce all the things necessary for life.
Indeed, for long periods of human history – hundreds
of thousands of years in fact – sorting out our food
and other living arrangements would take between
around fifteen and seventeen hours per week.[6] The
rest of our time would be spent on other pursuits.

Even just a few hundred years ago, before the rule
of capital, the survival of much of the population was
largely determined by the amount of work that needed
to be done. Peasants would cultivate the commons in
order to feed and clothe themselves and their families.
From the point of view of our clock-focused working
lives, the relationship between work and time in the
feudal period is unrecognisable: people toiled for as
long as was required upon and within the commons,
or provided a surplus for their masters in return for a
plot of their own. Work was governed very much by
seasonal cycles and traditional hierarchies of tribute
and ownership rather than contracted hours.[7]

Of course, we should hold no rose-tinted illusions
here. Life and work in the pre-capitalist era was far
from ideal. Though societies were not governed by the
clock of the boss, they were governed by things like
patriarchal kinship structures and other seemingly

immovable customs, in which the 'guild masters exploited journeymen, lords exploited serfs, men exploited women, the old exploited the young.'[8]

When labour productivity became the central imperative of the economy, these age-old relations began to be supplanted, or at least subsumed, by employer–employee relations. And so, capitalism – the production of goods for the realisation of value (and ultimately profit) – was born. This process caused a division between those who owned land or property and those who only owned the labour they could provide to others. As Raj Patel and Jason Moore put it:

> The creation of modern work happened in Europe through enclosure, a variegated process that trans-formed human relationships to the rest of nature and to the ways days were spent – even down to the way time was understood.[9]

The market – including the waged labour market – became the workplace for the majority of the population as land was taken away. At the same time, the state started to impose punishments for idleness and vagrancy.[10] This was a process of impoverishment and withdrawal of access to means of survival; it was simultaneously the creation of cheap labour in need of work – and therefore an opportunity for employers.[11] The ability to make people work for a regular payment for a living opened the doors to employers pushing workers to their physical limits – extending both the working week to exhausting lengths and even expanding the labour force by enlisting young children. The labour-obsessed society, that we still live in today, was born.

Ultimately, Marx's critique of work stems from a concern for human freedom and the forms of coercion that modern society imposes on the individual. His account of the emergence of waged employment alerts us to its ignoble origins and the basic fact that the logic of profit directs the lives of all who must engage in the labour market. Employment is therefore, in a fundamental sense, opposed to individual freedom: it means renting ourselves out to someone, or a company, for a certain amount of time.

With a strong sense of irony, Marx often referred to the 'free labourer' in order to capture the dual character of what it is to be an employee: you are 'free' insofar as you can 'choose' to sell yourself to work to whichever employer you want, and on the other hand you are also 'free' of things, insofar as you own nothing (or next to nothing) but your own ability to work. Today, Marx's description of the proletarian condition remains sadly relevant. One in four Brits have no savings in the bank, so are working from paycheck to paycheck with nothing but their labour to sell.[12]

Of course, neither of these things amount to anything like freedom – the freedom to use our time for what we will – and this is because, ultimately, for the vast majority of us who cannot live off inheritance or the assets we own, we need a job to pay for our survival (without one, we are 'free' to starve).

The tyranny of the workplace and human impoverishment

Beyond the logic of the labour market and the lack of freedom that this imposes on us, many social theorists have provoked us to pay close attention to that 'hidden abode' of Marx's we all know too well: the workplace. Here, you don't have to be a Marxist to see that this is not a sphere of freedom; why then would you want to spend so much time there?

Political philosopher Elizabeth Anderson draws parallels between the public governance exercised by states and the 'private government' exercised by managers in firms.[13] Using this analogy, she brings to light a number of uncomfortable truths about the extent to which we, as employees, are subject to the relatively unchecked domination of our bosses. We wouldn't (knowingly) tolerate such undemocratic, granular control of intimate aspects of our lives by the state, Anderson asks, so why should we take it for granted when it comes to our employer?

And yet, this is exactly what happens, every day, in those little islands of unfreedom that we call 'the office'. Our leaders (managers) are selected by the CEO or board, but not by their subordinates; we are told what we can wear, how our hair should look and who we can talk to; we are notified that our phone calls and emails at work are potentially being listened to; in many cases, even political activity outside of the job can function as a sanctionable offence by the boss. If we have had enough of these restrictive regimes, we can quit, you might say. But then where else do we have to turn to but another regime (workplace) of a different flavour, or else face the hardship of unemployment?

Even our lives outside of the home can come under scrutiny in the world of private government. If this sounds like far-fetched scaremongering, it isn't. Henry Ford famously set a precedent when he established a 'Sociological Department' at Ford in order to monitor his workforce's household cleanliness, their diets, their drinking habits and more.[14] Today, similar initiatives are not uncommon: under the Affordable Care Act (ACA), for example, US employers can impose penalties on those workers who do not comply with wellness programmes, which sometimes prescribe exercise and abstinence from alcohol.[15]

Anderson's main target of critique is the American labour market, which arguably has fewer bulwarks against employer power than other parts of the world. However, in the UK things are often not much better, with regular stories of draconian, intrusive measures taken by owners and managers against their staff. One of Britain's largest retailers, Sports Direct, for example, is infamous for using a whole set of disciplinary measures that could easily be confused with techniques utilised in prisons.[16] An undercover investigation found that rigorous strip searches, 'encouragements' over a loudspeaker to work harder and corrective threats of firing were all used. The parliamentary inquiry that followed likened these practices to those found in 'Victorian workhouses'.[17] Similar stories of intense managerial control have emerged from Amazon fulfilment centres, among other workplaces.[18]

The pressure, speed and surveillance of modern work inevitably takes its toll on workers. In fact, the intensification of work in the UK has been on an upward trend for decades. In 2017, 46 per cent of the British employed workforce strongly agreed that their jobs required them to work 'very hard'; this compares with some 32 per cent back in 1992.[19] In the same study, 55 per cent of women and 47 per cent of men reported that they 'always' or 'often' returned home from work exhausted; the numbers for those in nursing and teaching professions are even more stark.[20] The UK government's Health and Safety Executive reports that a record 17.9 million working days were lost due to work-related stress, depression or anxiety in 2019/20. This compares to 12.8 million in the previous year; a 40 per cent increase in cases. What was the predominant cause of these illnesses? Workload pressure, or more specifically 'tight deadlines, too much work or too much pressure'.[21]

All of the above, to be clear, come from a time *before* a global pandemic swept into UK workplaces, communities and domestic life. And what we see emerging subsequently paints an even grimmer picture of the impact that Covid has had. The pandemic has seen mental distress at work rise by 49 per cent when compared to the 2017/2019 period.[22]

Working time is clearly playing its part in this degradation of working life. A study carried out by the Mental Health Foundation suggested that among those working from home during the pandemic, an extra 28 hours per month were being worked on average, with clear negative impacts on health and well-being.[23] As large chunks of the workforce switch to remote working, the work–life barrier begins to break down: it is no longer possible to leave your work at the office when the office is constantly in your living room. For those 'key workers' remaining at their usual place of work – involving some of the most stressful jobs at the best of times – the usual workplace pressure now has the added threat of serious risk of infection.

Yet, the issue of working time – and our relationship to it – is not new, nor is it extraneous to how our economies and labour markets are organised. Marx was one of the first, and one of the most astute, critics of an economic system that presses us into long working hours and stressful workplaces, dominated by tight management protocols and maximised workloads. Working time cuts right to the heart of life within capitalism today, just as it did in the nineteenth century. Time is money, but time is also a precious resource for our freedom. The tug of war between time for ourselves and time for our employer is one that has never gone away.

As obvious as it may sound, as long as the profit motive drives the modus operandi of firms, the burden of productivity rests on staff – with every minute bearing the promise of greater profit. And while there are a minority of genuinely forward-thinking businesses that recognise the burdens that work places on their staff (and run shorter working weeks, decent holiday allowances and so on to compensate), these remain very much the exception to the rule. This is the inescapable truth that lies behind our work-centred lifestyles, our regular burnouts and the misery of not having a job and yet requiring one for survival.

2 – UNTAPPED POTENTIAL: LABOUR-SAVING TECHNOLOGY AND HUMAN FLOURISHING

The human choice is clear enough. Nobody who for any length of time has done heavy, dirty or dangerous labour, or for that matter endlessly repetitive routine impersonal tasks, could wish for anything but the further development of true labour-saving.[1]

Keynesian common sense

One of the most famous figures in the debate around working time in capitalism is John Maynard Keynes. Aside from carving out a formidable legacy in economic theory and practice, one that is still influential to this day, one of Keynes's most memorable, and oft-cited, texts is his 'Economic Possibilities For Our Grandchildren'.[2]

There, Keynes stressed that although humans have always used technology as part of their economic

life, in the modern period the development of tools
and technological innovations has exponentially
accelerated. With new technology have come vast
reductions in human labour time. Between 1870 and
1930 (when Keynes was writing), over 400 hours had
been knocked off the average working year in the
UK, equal to over seven hours taken off each working
week.[3] For Keynes, the meaning of this trend was
clear: with growth continuing at this pace, fewer and
fewer human hours were required to produce the
things we needed, and the working week would continue to shrink, perhaps to around fifteen hours by
the year 2030.

Keynes based this prediction on an account of
human need. Needs, he thought, fell into two camps.
Firstly, there are 'absolute' needs, which refer to the
baseline necessities common to all, 'whatever the situation of our fellow human beings' (e.g., shelter, food
and so on). Secondly, there is the need to 'satisfy the
desire for superiority'. Absolute needs, Keynes
believes, can be easily met: 'A point may soon be
reached, much sooner perhaps than we are all of us
aware of, when these needs are satisfied in the sense
that we prefer to devote our further energies to
non-economic purposes.'[4]

This prospect of meeting basic human needs, and
reducing the need for us to work, had philosophical,

perhaps even existential, repercussions for Keynes. It suggests that 'the economic problem is not – if we look into the future – the *permanent problem of the human race*'.[5] If we no longer have the challenge of trying to meet our material needs, we face entirely novel choices: what should we do with ourselves? What should a human being *be*?

Keynes was heavily influenced by ancient Greek ethics. His ideas about the good and the striving for the good in itself were influenced by Plato,[6] while the search for the good life was based on Aristotle's idea that economics is the use of what is necessary for life in general.[7] Indeed, in his view, economics would lead to the good, beautiful life if it were correctly utilised. For Keynes, working fewer hours and enjoying the 'good life' is associated with a conception of a life in which our finite quantity of material needs are satisfied.

According to a Keynesian point of view then, we should put back on the table the issue of ethics – what the purpose of economic activity is – together with appropriate policies or forms of investment that involve the arts, architecture, sports, education and other activities that people might wish to pursue in their versions of the good life.

Keynes's mistake:
underestimating 'economic rationality'
Yet this account leaves the obvious question begging:
why have we not achieved anything near the working
time reduction that Keynes predicted? Let's not forget
that in the UK we still work on average over forty
hours per week – some way off the fifteen that Keynes
was hoping for by 2030.[8]

Keynes's optimism about the growth of the economy
and the *distribution* of the benefits of this growth
both need addressing. With regards to the former, his
belief was not so misplaced: GDP per capita more
than quadrupled between the early 1930s and late
2000s in Western Europe and North America.[9] But if
economies in the Global North have become far
richer – as Keynes predicted – why have our working
weeks not been reduced in line with this increase?
This underlines the importance of distribution, and it
is here that the flaw in Keynes's optimism lies. In
truth, the correlation between greater productivity
and working time reduction in the decades around the
late nineteenth and early twentieth centuries was not
a result of an economic or natural 'law', but of growing political campaigns on the part of trade unions
and public figures for shorter hours.[10]

Indeed, Keynes wrote his provocation towards the
end of this period of remarkable trade union activity

in the UK following the First World War. Trade unions were campaigning hard for increased pay and shorter hours, with strike action common.[11] One of the greatest – and longest lasting – reductions in working time occurred in 1919 as the result of many years of union and worker campaigns.[12] This reduction, bringing the working week down to forty-eight hours for many, was even sustained during the tumultuous 1920s through regular demonstration of union strength.[13] It was this very practical activity of organised workers that achieved the vast reductions in working time that the UK saw in the late nineteenth and early twentieth century, not just the movement of the economy itself.

Yet it is precisely this same activity that is missing in Keynes's account of the march of progress. These productivity- and/or technology-driven narratives often overlook the nitty-gritty politics of distribution that make change happen. Without pressure – often from trade unions – the length of the working week could still well be somewhere around seventy hours per week. In contrast to an understanding that assumes that economics is about ever more efficient ways of meeting needs, these worker struggles over just who gets to see the benefits of greater productivity have shown us that profit and endless accumulation are just as – if not more – powerful imperatives that drive economic development.

Making technology work for freedom

Of course, Keynes's intuition about the ability to meet our needs with greater and greater ease was not wrong. Another use of labour-saving technology was, and is, entirely possible – even if this possibility is constrained by the 'economic rationality' that dominates our societies. Political philosopher Andre Gorz encapsulates this tension in his book *Capitalism, Socialism, Ecology*:

> The chief consequence of our drive towards efficiency and economic rationalization is that it frees us from work, frees up our time, releases us from the rule of economic rationality itself – an outcome which economic rationality is incapable either of evaluating or of endowing with meaning.[14]

Science and technology build our productive capacity, and this capacity opens up the possibility for freedom from work. And yet, this utopian scenario is foreclosed by the rationality that production is for profit and precisely *not* for meeting needs. Technical productivity points towards a world beyond productivity for profit.

This line of argument also motivates those from other strands of radical thought. In his re-reading of Freud's theory of civilisation for example, Hebert

Marcuse discusses the repression of desire and its potential liberation through the reduction of working hours:

> Since the length of the working day is itself one of the principal repressive factors imposed upon the pleasure principle by the reality principle, the reduction of the working day to a point where the mere quantum of labor time no longer arrests human development is the first prerequisite for freedom.[15]

Giving ourselves more time is not merely about liberation from a boss, but also the ground for new forms of desire to flourish. Should technology, in such a project, be directed toward the ends of human satisfaction, for example, then 'productivity loses its repressive power and impels the free development of individual needs.'[16] This is an argument – now quite familiar – for the merits of the automation of our labours and the liberation of our time and desires.[17] The necessity of earning a living weighs on us from early adulthood and continues right through to old age. Removing this burden by repurposing our productive capacity would be nothing short of civilisational change.

In essence then, certain elements of Keynes's common sense are worth hanging on to: the productivity gains from new technologies *could and should* lead to reduced working weeks. Beyond drastically reducing poverty and destitution (no small gain!), this would also provide us with the opportunity to ask ourselves what is most important and to act on it, to think beyond merely 'being productive' and ultimately to become fuller beings with broader horizons than simply making ends meet. But the lesson we should draw from history is that such an ideal situation will not emerge quasi-naturally, via the advance of productive technologies, but will have to be demanded, fought for and campaigned for across society.[18]

Untethering human potential

As Marx and many other analysts of the division of labour have argued, the vast majority of jobs under capitalism only develop human skills to the extent that they become useful to the business. You learn word processing so you can send those emails. You learn how to make lattes just so they can be sold. Your interpersonal skills are improved primarily to lubricate the day-to-day running of the firm. It is incredibly rare for workers to have the chance to develop themselves in a manner of their own choosing, with company finances, on company time. These circumstances only come about in high-income roles, often as perks with which to entice employees to remain in their job or to put up with intense moments of stress.

We spend our lives in jobs that give us very limited scope to develop ourselves, and which are specifically designed to be so routine that they can be picked up by almost anyone who gets hired. The time for our own fulfilment and development is elsewhere. Even the acknowledged – and consistently misinterpreted – father of modern economics, Adam Smith, was well aware of what the division, and standardisation, of tasks did to us as humans.[19] Alongside making us more productive as workers, he warns that '[t]he man whose whole life is spent in performing a few simple operations, of which the effects are perhaps always the same, or very nearly the same, has not occasion to exert his understanding.'[20]

Reducing our time at work is as much about human potential as it is about economic equality. Among those who saw the huge potential of a culture in which necessary labour was reduced to a minimum, British philosopher Bertrand Russell was one of the most prominent.

Even now, it is often only long hours that make work irksome. If the normal hours of work were reduced to (say) four, as they could be by better organisation and more scientific methods, a very great deal of work which is now felt as a burden would quite cease to be so.[21]

Russell was sifting through the philosophies of anarchism and socialism of his day, attempting to isolate their most promising ideas. He thought it was perfectly clear that, alongside financial security, the reduction of work time was truly the most emancipatory and desirable goal for mankind. To the accusation – often heard in conversations around work, deeply infused with the work ethic – that with less of our time spent in jobs we'd become an 'idle', or even lazy, society, Russell has this to say:

> Among those who would be classed as idlers might be included artists, writers of books, men devoted to abstract intellectual pursuits – in short, all those whom society despises while they are alive and honours when they are dead ... Whoever will observe how many of our poets have been men of private means will realise how much poetic capacity must have remained undeveloped through poverty; for it would be absurd to suppose that the rich are better endowed by nature with the capacity for poetry.[22]

This is an important rebuttal to anyone who claims that free time is a luxury, only of interest to the elite. This gets things the wrong way round, and at the same time merely state the obvious. Our most famous artists, writers and intellectuals often have wealthy backgrounds. They have been the ones who have had the means to be able to distance themselves from the daily grind of 'earning a living' and who can devote their energies to more creative pursuits. Russell should know – he himself was of the privileged minority who enjoyed the space and time to engage in these aspects of human life that we might call 'ends in themselves'. We can only imagine the wealth of art, music, poetry and cinema that has never seen the light of day because millions of individuals simply haven't had the time or material security to experiment freely. In this hypothetical scenario, the actually existing, working-class cultural production that has existed since at least the post-war period is merely a fraction of what would have been possible, had we been working anything near Keynes's dream of a fifteen-hour week.

Russell's celebration of creative, or we might say 'non-productive', activities, points to a broader philosophical point about the importance of free time. Twentieth-century writer Georges Bataille also lamented the work-centred society – common to both Western capitalism and Soviet communism – for its irrational and fundamentally *austere* way of ordering people's lives.[23] We work to survive, or, if we are lucky, to accumulate a surplus for our savings, which in turn are used to accumulate more for further survival. If we are fortunate enough to own a business, or own property, then all we have gained are new mechanisms for accumulating yet more, via the work and rent of others.

But what, Bataille asks, is the purpose of all this accumulation? When is the time for enjoyment? When can our everyday activities be ends in themselves, such as in play, in sex, in discovery and in the enjoyment of music, film and other arts? These 'sovereign' activities (as opposed to the servility of non-stop work) are often stigmatised as 'elitist', frivolous luxuries or quite simply a 'waste of time'. For Bataille, this is an extreme misinterpretation of the facts: it is modern, routine work that is void of meaning unless it forms the basis for a life beyond the constant grind.

A rebalancing of our priorities is required, from the work-centred society to one in which work competes with communal enjoyment, the free expenditure of our bodily energies and the exploration of human capacities hitherto unknown.

A question for socialists

The nature of work in industrial society, the pressures of workplace domination and the consequences of labour process standardisation sketched above should give us pause to consider what our preferred alternatives to capitalism would look like. If these institutional features of *capitalist* society are to be abolished in that society's overcoming, then socialism, communism, post-capitalism or whatever alternative name suits best does not just denote a shift in who owns the economy, the land it is built on or the organisations operating within it; nor does it merely imply changing what we produce and how the products of our labours are distributed – however necessary these changes are. A non- or post-capitalist society will also have to reckon with how we work and for how long.

In her path-breaking work on this topic, *The Problem With Work*, Kathi Weeks describes political projects devised under the remit of socialism as often having failed in providing an alternative political economy to capitalism beyond full employment and what she calls 'productivism'. Weeks identifies two different socialist visions of a post-capitalist future that share a commitment to labour as a fundamental human value and goal.[24]

The first, 'socialist modernization', is characterised by the attempt to fully realise the productive potential of the forces of production developed under capitalism.[25] Socialism would democratise the economic relations of ownership and control so that production was in the hands of the workers rather than the current capitalist class. Although ownership would, in theory at least, be freed from the imperative of profit for profit's sake, the means of production and the labour process would remain wedded to the industrial model born of capitalist relations. Capitalism is here seen as an inefficient way of organising the forces of modernity – one which will be set straight by the collective appropriation of the means of production.

Lenin's attitude towards capitalist work practices serves as an example of the socialist modernisation disposition. Before the Russian Revolution, Lenin was highly critical of the capitalist (Taylorist) regimentation of the workplace.[26] In 1913 he writes:

[Taylorism's] purpose is to squeeze out of the worker three times more labour during a working day of the same length as before; all the worker's strength is unmercifully roused, every bit of nervous and muscle energy is drained from the slave labourer at three times the speed . . . Advances in the sphere of technology and science in capitalist society are but advances in the extortion of sweat.[27]

However, in 1918 Lenin had modified his views in the context of post-revolutionary Russia, writing in the magazine *Pravda* that

> We should try out every scientific and progressive suggestion of the Taylor system . . . the Taylor System, as well as all progressive measures of capitalism, combine the refined cruelty of bourgeois exploitation and a number of most valuable scientific attainments in the analysis of mechanical motions during work.[28]

Taylorist control over workers is indeed a capitalist tool or coercion, but, Lenin writes, if 'properly controlled and intelligently applied by the working people themselves' it could become a crucial foundation of socialism.[29] For socialist modernists like Lenin,

> Socialism is seen as a new mode of politically administering and economically regulating the *same* industrial mode of producing to which capitalism gave rise; it is thought to be a social form of distribution that is not only more just, but also more *adequate* to industrial production.[30]

The key flaw in such a vision of socialism is of course that the nature and experience of work would barely

be different from that of the capitalist world we had
apparently left behind. Nick Dyer-Witheford goes as
far as to argue that 'Leninism should be understood
as a Marxism highly adapted – indeed, fatally
overadapted – to a particular moment of capitalist
development . . . with its Taylorist division of labor,
industrial mechanisation, and emphasis on "mass
organiation" '.[31] In socialist modernisation we find
'an endorsement of economic growth, industrial
progress, and the work ethic similar to the one that
can be found in bourgeois political economy, with its
naturalization and celebration of the processes of
economic modernization'.[32] Would we really be able
to say, under such a socialist system, that everyday life
was truly revolutionised if we had the similar workloads, similar productivity pressures and similar hours
as under capitalism, albeit with new bosses and different products?[33]

While socialist modernisation focuses on ownership and worker exploitation, socialist humanism, on
the other hand, is another variant of productivist
discourse that Weeks warns against. It proceeds from
the argument that, under capitalist labour conditions,
the individual is alienated from their human essence.
This perspective often rejects the technological capa-
bilities of modernity, as the labour process within this
model (under the guise of scientific rationalism) is too

tightly imbricated with the logic of capital accumulation, alienating humans from their 'natural' ways of
working.

To labour is instead understood, as Weeks explains,
as 'an individual creative capacity, a human essence
from which we are now estranged and to which we
should be restored'.[34] For socialist humanists, one of
the central tenets for counteracting the ills of capitalism, therefore, is not more or less work, but better
work. The goal for socialism should be to restore
work's dignity and worth, rather than contesting its
status as the central pillar of social value.[35]

The problem with this reading of socialism, for
Weeks, is that it 'preserves too many of capitalism's
structures and values' – namely, the 'work dogma'
that tells us that work is one of the highest goods.[36]
Socialist humanism does not have room, she argues,
for the demand for working less, as it understands
work as fundamentally part of the human's essence.

It's possible to detect, as Weeks does, a tendency
here towards nostalgia and the romanticisation of
certain forms of pre-industrial labour – namely craft
production.[37] Reuniting the human with itself via
work entails closing the loop between production and
consumption, which lends itself to work that produces
objects of immediate consumption: farming, the
crafting of tools and so on. Beyond the question of

the feasibility of such a vision of the future, we might question whether it is truly far enough away from the labour-obsessed society that we currently experience.

> The affirmation of unalienated labor is not an adequate strategy by which to contest contemporary modes of capitalist control; it is too readily co-opted in a context in which the metaphysics of labor and moralization of work carry so much cultural authority in so many realms.[38]

In the humanist rejection of capitalism, in other words, critique often does not extend to capitalism's obsession with labour itself, and thus does not account adequately for Marx's insistence that freedom requires a shortening of the working day. By extolling the virtues of work as central to the project, socialist humanist visions allow themselves to fall into the comfortable – but dangerously capitalist – niche of exonerating work for works' sake.

Weeks's analysis then, among others,[39] reveals that it isn't only the ideology of capitalism that moralises, normalises and mythologises work: the adoration of work infiltrates variants of socialism and some 'traditional' Marxist discourses too. This raises a question for socialists today: what kind of working life should be envisaged beyond the present? There is so much that is wrong with the labour process in capitalist economies, and the quantity of time we spend at work is right at the heart of them. Although it is not controversial to demand better and more purposeful work for ourselves, bolder and more fundamental transformation is required if we are truly to leave behind the woes of work that our industrial/post-industrial workscapes impose upon us. Working time reduction, we proffer, has to be part of the next economic system.

Of course, this debate isn't – and shouldn't be – solely theoretical. In truth, the majority of working people are regularly in favour of shortening their working weeks, and trade unions have consistently made working time one of their priorities in negotiations with employers.[40] Multiple polls of both the UK and abroad in recent years show an overwhelming preference for working four days (or fewer) instead of the standard five.[41] When the Trades Union Congress polled thousands of UK workers in 2018, over three-quarters of respondents were clear that they wanted to work four days or fewer.[42] During the Covid pandemic, this desire for fewer hours has been maintained, with 63 per cent of people in the UK supporting the idea when asked in the summer of 2020; only 12 per cent opposed. It seems that the shorter working week is an idea whose time has come.

3 – WOMEN'S TIME AND THE SHORTER WORKING WEEK

> We don't have to prove that we can 'break the blue collar barrier.' A lot of us have broken that barrier a long time ago and have discovered that the overalls did not give us any more power than the apron – quite often even less, because now we had to wear both and had even less time and energy to struggle against them. The things we have to prove are our capacity to expose what we are already doing as work, what capital is doing to us, and our power to struggle against it.[1]

While we all live in a world obsessed with labour, not all of us experience it equally. Those who live at the sharp end of capitalism, in racialised populations, or those who live and work in the Global South for instance, generally experience worse working conditions and lower incomes, and disproportionately occupy the more precarious and undesirable parts of the labour market.[2] We are all unequal under a capitalist economy; but some are more unequal than others. The same is true for women and the ways in which the pressures of the world of work intersect with gender norms. Here again, free time (or its lack) emerges as a precious resource, and one that modern working life denies to many women.

Home is where the heart is
A gendered division of labour is intrinsic to capitalism. As market-based relations spread over and through feudal society, 'economic' production was moved into factories and offices and remunerated with wages, while reproductive labour,[3] on the other hand, was relegated to a demarcated private sphere, becoming naturalised as an activity carried out in the name of 'love' and 'virtue'.[4] The modern, private household, 'the principal institutional basis for women's subordination in capitalist societies', as it is called by feminist thinker, Nancy Fraser, was established.[5] The labours of the domestic sphere were reclassified as moral, unproductive duties, separate from the remunerated economic sphere of waged labour that became coded as the driver of industrial society. From roughly the seventeenth century onwards, a woman's remit became the organisation of the home, on the one hand, and the care and

cultivation of their children (future workers), on the other.[6]

While in theory these two spheres are distinct, they are, and have been for some time, co-dependent on one another. The family's financial survival was won by the employed sweat of the man's brow; and in turn, the strains and traumas of employed work (during the Industrial Revolution, that meant no weekends, long days and very few rights) required a domestic 'lattice of protection – a truly human, flesh and blood safety net', as class historian Jeremy Seabrook frames it, to receive the male workers in recovery.[7]

This function of women in the wider economy was, and still is, common to all classes. In her history of the housewife, Catherine Hall notes a similar development in the emerging middle class family of the nineteenth century:

> One of the major functions of the Victorian family was to provide a privatised haven for the man who was subject day in and day out to the pressures of competition in the new industrial world.[8]

Whether it was at the coalface or in the accounting house, the male breadwinner required (and expected) a home, food on the table and someone to care for the children. This continued to be thought of as a woman's role into the twentieth century, when, during the 1950s, the housewife ideal, as Lynne Pettiger notes, 'seemed both ordinary and aspirational'.[9] She continues:

> [Housewives] got the dubious bonus of being framed not as working but fulfilling natural urges by caring – morally valuable in the sense that it had to be done, but not valuable in the way that production is valuable.[10]

All of these domestic roles involve, of course, work. Yet this work goes unaccounted for and often unrecognised, hidden by the 'natural' role women occupy in modern life.[11] That is, the unpaid work of the home is 'not *economically* valuable, which in a capitalocentric world is the value that counts'.[12]

Employment, gender and time
If the history of capitalism has been intimately involved with the creation and demarcation of the gendered, unpaid work of care, cleaning and the bringing-up of children, all underpinning the traditionally male-dominated world of employment, how have things changed in more recent decades? During the twentieth century, powerful demands for greater civic rights and for financial independence, as well as the experience of two world wars, during which

women were brought into the labour force to replace men at the front, began to blur the spheres of what work was 'proper' to men and to women. Women gradually entered a wider range of workplaces, and in ever greater numbers. Labour market participation rates for women in Britain, for instance, rose from 29 per cent in 1985 to 44 per cent in 2017, and globally, women now represent just under 40 per cent of the total workforce.[13]

Gender norms have proven difficult to shift, however, even as women have moved from the unpaid workplace of the home to the commodified workplaces of industry. That is to say, women remain the primary carers, cleaners and emotional labourers of the economy, despite the achievements of the women's equality movement. In the UK, to take an indicative example, 88 per cent of nurses, 84 per cent of teachers and 83 per cent of care workers are women.[14] And just as it was when hidden from view in the black box of the private household, socially reproductive work such as in these examples is systematically undervalued, despite its huge social importance. Care workers, nursery assistants, pharmacy assistants and other female-dominated occupations all pay wages that on average fall below the recognised poverty line.[15]

During the global Covid-19 pandemic, the gender inequalities within the labour market became even

more starkly visible. Many female – or rather feminised – occupations involve close contact and often
'high-touch' tasks that put those performing them at
huge risk of contracting and spreading such a con-
tagious and deadly virus. A study carried out by the
Autonomy think tank ranked occupations according
to the extent that physical proximity and day-to-day
exposure to illnesses were part of the work. As Covid
is a virus that spreads through breath and particles
passing between people in the air and on surfaces, the
study can act as a general guide to which kinds of
jobs might come into contact with Covid the most. It
found that 77 per cent of the workforce who have
'high-risk' jobs are women, and that women make up
a staggering 98 per cent of workers in high-risk jobs
that are being paid poverty wages.

The devalued nature of many feminised occupations means that women are also more susceptible to
job insecurity and precarity. Liberal politicians of the
early 2000s attempted to address the pronounced time
burdens of women through initiatives that promoted
'work–life' balance. Although the use of the term was
adopted and accelerated by elements of the women's
liberation movements of the 1960s,[16] its descendent,
neoliberal reimagining pivots away from visions of
collective emancipation for women and towards a
more individualised relationship between employer

and worker. A major part of this project, and one that still retains the promise of genuine progress, was the invention of 'flexible' working.[17] The progressive ambition at its core is the idea that the time required for the job might fit around the demands of the employee's life.

The grim reality of 'flexibility' in today's labour market is well documented, however. Employers have used malleable contract terms, such as those with no minimum guaranteed hours (zero-hours contracts) and bogus self-employment in order to be able to hire and fire individuals more easily, and avoid providing many of the benefits that employees on standard contracts enjoy.[18] Women account for over half of workers on such zero-hours contracts in the UK, making precarious flexibility – or one-sided flexibility – a gendered issue.[19] Once again, the caring professions stand out for all the wrong reasons. In the UK, 35 per cent of care workers operate on zero-hours contracts.[20]

This continued undervaluing of paid care work is even more stark when understood in the context of the shifting industrial composition in the UK and beyond. As Helen Hester has argued, while the social imaginary remains fixated on masculinised workplaces such as the factory, the warehouse or the construction site, a large (and continually growing) portion of wealthier economies is centred around reproductive *waged* labour.[21] In fact, according to Hester and Srnicek's research, socially reproductive roles across healthcare, education, food services, accommodation and social work currently make up 23–8 per cent of the labour force in G7 countries.[22] To put this in perspective, at its peak in the 1960s, only 30 per cent of the American workforce worked in manufacturing.[23] While rapidly ageing populations mean that our economies will continue to become increasingly 'caring' in their make-up,[24] the pay and conditions of the largely female care workforce leave much to be desired.

The double-shift and the time poverty of women
Not only has the entry of women into labour markets not brought about the feminist utopia that the 'lean in' discourse claims it can,[25] but the required house-work and childcare necessary for life has not gone anywhere. Unpaid reproductive labour is still pre-dominantly carried out by women, often alongside the jobs that they now hold. Rather than being freed from the toil of unremunerated housework, women are now expected to perform both 'productive' and reproductive labour roles.

The Office for National Statistics (ONS) has shown that in 2016, women in the UK carried out 60 per cent more unpaid work than men.[26] The same study also revealed that women provided 74 per cent of all child-care time and spent, on average, twenty-six hours a week doing unpaid domestic labour. Men, in comparison, spend sixteen hours a week doing such unpaid work.[27] This is what sociologists have referred to as the second and third shifts: the structural way in which women are disproportionately burdened with having to engage in paid employment, domestic labour and emotional care work.[28]

Thus, not only are the kinds of jobs that women tend to occupy are indeed prone to stress, burnout and exhaustion, this pressure is further compounded by the persistent expectation of unpaid domestic work that women still face. As Deborah Hargreaves argues, women as employees have had to adapt and fit into a world of employment designed for individuals who simply do not have these unpaid work burdens: 'The workplace has been set up by men to fit a male career pattern . . . there has been little fundamental structural change in the western world for over 100 years.'[29]

The currently generally accepted working hours and patterns of work, in particular, are a prime symptom of this skewed and gendered set-up, structured as they are around male workers who have very few expectations placed on them to carry out reproductive

work in addition to their jobs. Reflecting on those
male trade unionists who fought for and won the
eight-hour working day in the early twentieth century,
Kathi Weeks muses that 'had [they] been held respon-
sible for unwaged domestic labor, it is difficult to
imagine that [they] could credibly have been expected
to work a minimum of eight hours a day.'[30]

Again, the Covid crisis has shone a light on this
gendered inequality of time. Studies have shown
that 86 per cent of women carrying out a standard
working week alongside childcare responsibilities
during the first phase of the pandemic experienced
some form of mental health problems.[31] A report,
carried out by think tanks Compass and Autonomy
and the 4 Day Week Campaign, also found that
women are 43 per cent more likely than men to have
increased their hours beyond a standard working
week during Covid.[32] The new world of work,
epitomised by working remotely from home, has
been experienced by women as a further deprivation
of time.

Wages for housework: time for ourselves
In her highly influential pamphlet *Wages Against
Housework,* Sylvia Federici summed up the aims of
the movement of the same name.[33] Recognising that
the gendered cage of housework represents 'the most

pervasive manipulation, and the subtlest violence of modern capitalism', she and her peers sought an end to it via a demand for payment; this was a redefinition and a revaluation, 'demystifying and subverting the role to which women have been confined in capitalist society'.[34]

The demand for 'wages for housework' had, ultimately, less to do with the money itself and more to do with denaturalising and detaching housework from femininity. As Federici said: 'It is the demand by which our nature ends and our struggle begins.'[35] Crucially, to demand a wage for the invisibilised work of the home is to make this work 'count', to make it sit side by side with socially recognised work that appears on the balance sheets. If we adjusted our perspective in such a way – and this is the revolutionary turn of the Wages for Housework (WfH) movement – then our economy (and our lives with it) would have to be turned upside down.

The WfH provocation functions in a very similar way with respect to time. The work of the household is, after all, valid labour time in the WfH view. Forcing society (but particularly those occupying the nodes of political and economic power) to confront the time of childcare, the time of food preparation and that of housework as legitimate working time would represent a revolutionary shift. What would have to be the

case, for example, for a single mother to be able to work
no more than a forty-hour week, if we had to account
for a full-time job and her family responsibilities
combined? How much of her work would have to be
redistributed to others? How much would she have
to be paid for all these labour hours, now that they are
all recognised as economically valuable?

The tools of social science can be of use here.
Sociologists have regularly tried to quantify the
economic value of social reproduction, with Margaret
Reid's early work in the 1930s leading the way.[36] Using
time-use diaries over many years, researchers at the
Centre for Time Use at University College London
have made more recent estimations.[37] They calculate
the economic value of hitherto unpaid working time
based on the cost of equivalent 'replacement' labour
hours of professional childcarers, laundry and dry-
cleaning occupations, nursery school teachers and so
on (all those jobs that perform for a wage what workers in the home do currently for free). Multiplying the
going market rate of these labours by the amount of
unpaid hours recorded by the UK population, 'yields
an estimate of the total value of time devoted to
unpaid work of about £26 billion in 1975 and £449
billion in 2015, respectively'.[38] This means that a
staggering 25 per cent of UK GDP is simply made up
of the shadow labours of the home,[39] and that is not

including the cost of the raw materials of this work and other intermediary goods.[40]

Feminist struggles around housework (struggles that remain pertinent to this day) are in this sense struggles around the recognition of invisible or 'deleted' working time. But the more radical figures of this movement such as Federici also take this one step further: the recognition of the value of this work is a stepping stone to reducing it. As Federici declares, 'we want money for each moment of it, so that we can refuse some of it and eventually all of it.'[41] Here, the fight for free time intersects with the feminist demand for revaluation; the fight for the control over time is at the same time the fight for gender equality.

Towards a fairer sharing of work and time

What's clear is that the modern world of work, and the 'official' labour market, were created under gendered forms of inequality, and that they have profound consequences for the experiences of time that persist today. Women get a raw deal on both fronts: they remain burdened with the majority of the unpaid care work that forms the backbone of society *and* they are faced with inferior working conditions to men in the world of paid work.

Addressing these forms of inequality involves redefining, as a society, the way we work, and also changing how long we work for. This translates into *reducing* the amount of hours defined as full-time employment in order to take into account the work that we know goes on outside of the labour market. By reducing the employed working week for all, you open up space for a fairer distribution of domestic tasks between men and women: the 'second shift' can become a more equal 'job share'. Further, reducing employment hours might also relieve pressure on those workers who suffer particularly from burnout and stress. As we have seen, workers in this category include teachers and nurses, who overwhelmingly tend to be women. The demand for a shorter working week thus recognises both the disproportionate toll employment takes on the health of female workers, while also providing more time for the work of care that is required at home.[42]

Reducing the working hours of women can take other forms too: extending or allowing the reallocation of paternity leave as a universal right is a positive direction in this regard. Allowing men to take extended periods of time off paid work to care for newborn children, or alternatively creating the opportunity in which to reallocate maternity leave to the father, would provide the foundation for denaturalising the maternal role of the mother as the primary caregiver.[43] This might also provide the opportunity for mothers, if they choose, not to have the forced break from employment that can hinder career promotions and increases in pay.

In addition to reducing the working week, we also need to consider more structural and infrastructural changes to our work *spaces* that can help reduce the time burden of unpaid domestic work. Proposals for the socialisation and redistribution of care work and other, currently home-bound, activities fits into a rich history of feminist theory. Community kitchens, cooked food services, homes without kitchens and towns without housework were just some of the radical ideas popularised by the materialist feminist movement of the nineteenth century.[44] These ideas have been taken up contemporarily in proposals for new public forms of infrastructure. Long Term Care Centres (the establishment of a space outside of the home and in the community and built around the overlapping needs of different kinds of carers and care-receivers) and community open workspaces, are more recent indications of the ways in which working time can be diffused throughout communities and not concentrated within private household units, ultimately to fall on one person's shoulders.[45]

Shorter working weeks should be a central aim for progressive movements of working people in the twenty-first century, but the definition of worker must

also take the feminist challenge seriously if it is going
to be achieved. If our aim is equality in the workplace,
we must understand the workplace as being more
than simply the office, the warehouse or the factory;
we must remember that our economy, our families
and our lives are underpinned by typically unpaid or
poorly paid forms of caring labour carried out
predominantly by women in domestic spaces. We
need to recognise that women are also at the sharp
end of the labour market, working in often precarious
jobs. And ultimately, we must acknowledge the reali-
ties of the double and triple shifts and work towards
ways of redistributing this work so we can all work less.

4 – TIME FOR THE ENVIRONMENT

> The commitment to an alternative politics of prosperity based on a sustainable economic order needs to be seen as a continuation of the emancipatory project. If we have a cosmopolitan care for the well-being of the poor of the world, and a concern about the quality of life for future generations, then we have to campaign for a change of attitudes to work, consumption, pleasure, and self-realisation in affluent communities.[1]

The debate around how we as a species move towards ecologically sustainable ways of living (i.e., within our planetary limits) is perhaps the most pressing discussion of our times.[2] Here, alongside questions of economic inequality, freedom and gender equality that we've explored in previous chapters, the shorter working week has a crucial role to play. In a simple formulation: working less is both necessary and desirable from an environmental perspective.

Changing the metrics

With climate breakdown already at our doorstep, the pressing need to change course from capitalist models of growth has spawned new disciplines and approaches within the field of economics. One such approach is referred to as degrowth – a genre of research and activism that has been active for many decades,[3] originally inspired by the political ecology of Gorz. Those who advocate for degrowth define its approach as being first and foremost a critique of growth.[4] Economic growth is unsustainable per se, because it is inseparable from greenhouse gas emissions and other negative environmental impacts.[5] In contrast to accounts that stress the need for 'green growth' or 'socialist growth',[6] degrowth advocates demand the dethroning of growth as a goal, and in its place, installing a political economy focused on using fewer natural resources in order to organise life and work.[7]

Rather than advancing an economic model destined for austerity, scarcity and recession (the socio-economic consequences usually associated with a flat or non-growing economies), degrowth and post-growth advocates argue in favour of economic metrics and objectives that advance alternative modes of living, based on principles of sharing, conviviality, care and the common good. As leading ecological economist Giorgos Kallis and his colleagues summarise:

Sustainable degrowth may be defined as an equitable downscaling of production and consumption that increases human well-being and enhances ecological conditions at the local and global level, in the short and long term. The adjective sustainable does not mean that degrowth should be sustained indefinitely but rather that the process of transition/transformation and the end-state should be sustainable in the sense of being environmentally and socially beneficial. The paradigmatic proposal of degrowth is therefore that human progress without economic growth is possible.[8]

A transition to degrowth must involve abandoning GDP (Gross Domestic Product) as a measure of success for an economy, and fundamentally recalibrating what we value. In short: change the metrics. Rather than viewing perpetual growth as an end in itself, a sustainable degrowth approach would implement measurements that are geared towards, and that capture, societal well-being, ecological sustainability and social equality.[9]

Reducing our carbon footprint by working less
For advocates of degrowth, the transition to a new economy will be undergirded by a range of policy measures that actively encourage economic activity

based on resource *circulation* rather than resource *extraction*.[10] These tend to include a basic income (creating an income floor irrespective of an individual's earnings or employment status), a wide range of universal services (free public transport, housing, healthcare and education) and a high rate of tax and regulation on private assets (encouraging lower levels of consumerism and more environmentally sustainable uses of energy and resources).

One of the key components of a degrowth programme relates to working time and its reduction.[11] Working less not only reduces the sheer amount of resources being used as part of the labour process, but it also reduces the amount of carbon-intensive consumption that comes with what Juliet Schor calls the 'work and spend' cycle.[12] In a study that assessed the environmental impacts of twenty-seven Organisation for Economic Co-operation and Development (OECD) countries, Schor and her colleagues estimated that reducing our working hours by a quarter could reduce our carbon footprint by as much as 30 per cent.[13] For the average British worker, this would mean cutting our weekly forty-two hours of work to just over thirty-one hours – or, a four-day week.

In the US, a degrowth-inspired study evaluated the carbon footprint held by individual items consumed by households with shorter or longer hours. In short, each item of expenditure per household, reported via surveys, was ranked according to how carbon-intensive its production was – from packaged meals to pieces of clothing and so on. Their conclusion? '[H]ouseholds with longer work hours have significantly larger carbon footprints', demonstrating a worrying corre-lation between increasingly unsustainable consumption and high workload lifestyles.[14] This study is consonant with anecdotal everyday experience, where early starts and late finishes bequeath takeaway meals delivered by moped, ready meals thrown into the microwave because we're too tired to cook or an early morning breakfast deal wrapped in layers of plastic.

These findings underline an important facet of the argument for reduced hours: we must have a signifi-cant reduction in our working time, not only because the work we do is so carbon intensive, but also because of the consumption that occurs at the fringes of our working lives.

The Green New Deal:
an opportunity for better working lives
The advocates of degrowth have made valuable con-tributions, not least in highlighting the problematic aspects of the pursuit of economic growth. Yet, an ardent commitment to degrowth often fails to account for the ways in which certain areas of the

economy will need to *grow* very quickly in order to cut carbon emissions at the rates required. As economist Robert Pollin has argued, the key objective for governments around the world should be to decouple consumption from fossil fuels at both the macro and micro levels (in consonance with degrowth arguments) while *also* investing massively in green energy infrastructure as its replacement.[15] The net result of this could well be that economies (GDP) grow rapidly while still advancing a viable climate-stabilisation project.[16] This adds nuance to green strategy: the problem isn't necessarily growth per se, but specifically *which* areas of the economy grow, and to what extent.

Other critics of degrowth point to the strategy's lack of political nous. It is hard to find within degrowth an implementable or politically viable strategy that acknowledges issues of political governance, power relations and consent-building.[17] Although degrowth modelling shows that work *could* be redistributed on a macro level to all workers in the form of work-sharing, it tends to lack any detailed plans for *how* this could be actually implemented, even at the national scale (leaving global degrowth aside for a moment). Questions also remain, for example, around the situation of those who currently work in industries that would need to be abolished under a sustained degrowth strategy, or around the safeguards (if they are at all possible) that will need to be in place to protect wages as the economy shrinks.

If degrowth economics largely remains at the – still undoubtedly useful – level of economic calculation and critique, then a green *political* strategy that might succeed in implementing the necessary reforms is still some way off. One of the most exciting and tangible political developments that might change this, however, is the idea of a 'Green New Deal' (GND). While the GND is very much a concept under construction – as evidenced by the multitude of iterations in the world[18] – its origins can be traced back to *New York Times* journalist Thomas L. Friedman. In an article entitled 'A Warning from the Garden', Friedman argued that in order to reverse climate change, an industrial and fiscal strategy that matched the ambition of the Roosevelt administration was required.[19] Ann Pettifor, in her book *The Case for the Green New Deal*,[20] shows how Colin Hines, a Greenpeace staffer and campaigner, then took up the challenge outlined by Friedman by commissioning a report that proposed in detail what a GND would consist of.[21] In the report, a GND would be a framework of joined-up policy proposals that aims to address the 'triple crunch of the credit crisis, climate change and high oil prices'.[22]

While the GND demands economic and ecological system change at national and international levels – reforms that would fundamentally revolutionise approaches to finance, the global economy and planetary ecosystems[23] – its ambitions for the world of work leave much to be desired.[24] Comparing the current proposals for a GND to Roosevelt's original New Deal of the 1930s is revealing in this regard. There, we find precedents for the kind of considerations for the well-being of workers in the midst of a crisis contained within its path-breaking labour market reforms that would be required today. The Fair Labour Standards Act (1938), for example, established a normal working week of forty hours and a minimum wage.

Behind these reforms was Frances Perkins, the first woman ever appointed to the US cabinet and an ardent campaigner for workers' rights and for gender equality.[25] A few years prior to this legislation, in the heart of the Great Depression, came the 'President's Reemployment Agreement', effectively a seal of approval from the very top that encouraged firms to reduce the average workweek and to raise hourly wage rates.[26] These reforms and others like it offered American workers a new collective sense of freedom and prosperity, changing their world of work for the better. In so doing, the New Deal managed to articulate a new vision of the future by turning the crisis of the Wall Street crash into an opportunity for lasting change. Today, our own visions must, at the very least, match the ambition of Roosevelt and his team.

With this in mind, what do today's GND proposals offer in terms of radical transitions and inspiring plans, more than eighty years down the line from the original New Deal? What are the aspirations for workers under a Green New Deal? Or, in other words, what is the *new deal* aspect of the GND and what ambitions do GND advocates harbour for working time reduction?

The answers we can find to these questions are thin on the ground. One of the central pillars of the US version of a GND consists of a jobs guarantee – a policy proposal aimed at providing a universal solution to the dual problems of unemployment and low wages.[27] A jobs guarantee is a policy framework whereby the government is obliged to provide a job to whoever wants one.[28] Premised on a commitment to leave nobody behind during radical reshaping and transformation of the economy over such a short period of time, it has thus become a central pillar of many versions of the GND. In doing so, it attempts to provide both a mechanism for addressing those whose livelihoods would be adversely affected by a GND (for example, people working in carbon-intensive industries) while also strengthening worker power (the jobs created under a GND would be unionised and permit collective bargaining).

In the US version, as outlined by Alexandria Ocasio-Cortez, a jobs guarantee programme is constructed under the remit of three key pledges: 1) the creation of millions of good, high-wage jobs; 2) the provision of unprecedented levels of security and prosperity for all people of the US; 3) counteraction of systemic forms of injustice.[29] However, although a jobs guarantee could address some of the fundamental issues affecting workers today (precarious, low-skill and poorly paid work), it rarely gives any consideration to the relationship between sustainability and working time that is so prevalent in degrowth economics.

Similar issues play out in the interpretation of the GND in UK politics. In the 2019 general election, the Labour Party decided to recontextualise the GND under the banner of a 'Green Industrial Revolution'. Putting aside the feasibility of a green industrialism and its ability to sustain 'good' jobs on a mass scale, we have to question the *desirability* of re-envisioning the working and social conditions associated with nineteenth-century industrialism. As we saw in the introduction, Engels's investigation into the conditions of working-class life in Victorian England paints a bleak picture of social deprivation, inequality and extreme forms of exhaustion; industrialism tends towards overwork and exploitation.

There is a tendency, in short, exemplified by both the jobs guarantee and the green industrial strategy, for advocates of a GND to aggrandise labour and labouring within its green strategy. One example we can draw on here is Ann Pettifor's *The Case for the Green New Deal* (2019), in which she argues that the GND economy will 'be labour-intensive', due to the shortfall created by switching from the highly efficient fossil fuel energy to less efficient renewable energy. She also goes on to detail how 'activities that cannot be powered by the sun's energy will be undertaken by human energy: labour.'[30] The British GND, she says, will 'mobilise a "carbon army" of workers to under- take and maintain the transformation'.[31]

With such proclamations, the GND strays close to the 'socialist modernization' that, as we saw in an earlier chapter, Kathi Weeks cautions us against. Doesn't the promise of a military-scale, labouring society lose sight of jobs as means to ends, as necess- ary (but not necessarily desired) instruments which afford people the capacity to pursue their interests? As with the early Soviet dreams of mass Taylorised production, a labour-intensive GND risks adopting many of the central tenets of the capitalist production system – not least its irrational worth ethic.

Pettifor has aspirations that the work created by a GND will be meaningful due to the work being underpinned with 'skills, training and higher education'. As she says, 'The promise of the GND is that the workforce will be rewarded with meaningful tasks; resourced with skills, training and higher education.'[32]

While no one can argue with the aim of the creation of 'meaningful jobs' or 'gaining skills', such terms sound hollow to the ears of those who have heard the promises of 'employability' and 'upskilling' since at least the New Labour years.[33] Can we really expect the millions of newly-created GND jobs to be meaningful and fulfilling, somehow turning around centuries of standardisation, routinisation and managerial discipline that are the hallmarks of modern labour markets? Will work under a GND – whether it is rewilding landscapes, retrofitting homes, maintaining energy infrastructure and so on – not involve arduous, repetitive, standardised and managed work too? Following Smith, Keynes, Marx, Russell and the everyday experience of countless millions of workers over the past few centuries, we remain sceptical about plans that claim to be able to eliminate the pains of work simply by changing one's profession and by having greater job security.[34]

In short, the Green New Deal fails to tackle one of the key issues that remain when it comes to its vision of the new society. Critics such as Sharachandra Lele emphasise that without considerations of 'multi-dimensional wellbeing', Green New Deal positions are at risk of becoming single-minded programmes that maintain the spirit and practices of industrialism by prioritising merely mass job creation at best, and – at worst – GDP growth.[35] Lest we forget, neither environmental sustainability nor job creation in and of themselves are sufficient for a 'good society'. The key is to couple these with individual well-being (including freedom), collective equality and the ongoing sustainability of these things across generations.[36]

Working less is both necessary and desirable
From our point of view, degrowth, post-growth and Green New Deal strategies all demonstrate the need to place working time reduction at the centre of any post-carbon political economy. And not only does such a reduction offer a relatively simple and effective way of reducing carbon emissions, it also provides a clear purpose and vision to the new economy we so badly need – one built on both environmental and social justice. Although the content of a Green New Deal is still being worked out, in both its international and national contexts, it offers the most promising political and economic means for achieving a post-carbon political economy

beyond neoliberalism and perhaps beyond capitalism itself.

This, however, does not mean abandoning strategies of degrowth or post-growth economics, but instead incorporating them into the development of GND political programmes. In this sense, we must avoid simply understanding degrowth and GND approaches as a binary choice that renders their synthesis impossible. Coalition-building across environmental economics and progressive political movements could help to articulate how transitioning to a post-carbon economy appeals to the ways in which capitalism perpetuates not only environmental injustice, but also social and economic injustices on a planetary or universal scale.

Although still in their infancy, some GND proposals are cottoning on to why working time reduction is both an environmental and social justice policy. The Green New Deal for Europe initiative (GNDE) proposes a (green) Public Works programme (in the same vein as the original New Deal) involving mass retrofitting of homes, investment in worker cooperatives and in repair and reuse facilities. The millions of jobs required by such a transformation will, in the GNDE plan, involve shorter working weeks, acting as a pioneer for the rest of Europe's labour markets to follow. This chimes with the arguments of various degrowth and post-growth economists:[37] reducing working time could be a key strategy for redistributing wealth and avoiding mass unemployment.

Equally, it is inspiring to see prominent GND advocates Kate Aronoff and Thea Riofrancos pushing for reduced working time as part of their core set of GND demands.[38] Although the authors still maintain the need for a jobs guarantee, they are well aware of the woes of the contemporary workplace – 'the domination of the workplace still keeps most of us unfree'[39] – and see the obvious benefits of working time reduction being part of green political strategy:

Under a radical Green New Deal, with efficiency gains and automation controlled by people rather than bosses, we could meet everyone's needs working far less than we currently do – and we should. Study after study shows that shorter workweeks lower carbon footprints – the shorter the better. To cut carbon, we need to work less and share the remaining work more evenly.[40]

Instead of reducing the number of hours *some* people work in order to maintain jobs and wages (the conventional economic approach seen in times of capitalist recessions or depressions), work would be shared by reducing the working time of *all* workers, thereby expanding free time for all while avoiding unemployment or underemployment for some. Such a strategy would also help the necessary transition workers will need to make, from resource-intensive industries that will require winding down to more sustainable forms of work.

If we are to offer a new political economy – one that aims to deliver both social and environmental justice – a Green New Deal should not only promote job security and higher wages, but also reduce the amount of time we spend on the job: 'Redefining work is crucial – but so is reducing it.'[41] The Green New Deal is an opportunity to recast the economy in a way that treats workers as complete, rounded human beings, with capacities far exceeding the drudgery and monotony of working life. Above all, a shorter working week imbues the GND with that key ingredient of any political project: hope and desire for a better life. There is a huge opportunity here that green movements have yet to properly exploit.[42] Aronoff et al. once again:

> Carbon-free leisure doesn't just mean wholesome hobbies like hiking and gardening – we're firm believers in eco-friendly hedonism. Give us time for long dinners with friends and plenty of organic wine; outdoor adventures enhanced by legal weed grown and harvested by well-paid agricultural

workers; skinny-dipping in lakes that reflect moon and starlight.[43]

Reducing the working week must be one of the key components of this post-carbon economy for the two reasons we have argued for: it is a low-cost, high-impact instrument for reducing carbon emissions and would demonstrably improve working and social life. In that sense, a GND with less work is both necessary and desirable.

5 – THE STRUGGLE FOR THE SHORTER WORKING WEEK

Workers have always been more than mere proletarians ... workers are also parents who are concerned about the future of their children, men and women who are concerned about their dignity, autonomy, and growth as human beings, neighbours who are concerned about their community, and empathetic people who were concerned with social justice, civic rights, and freedom.[1]

When faced with the multiple crises that have emerged in the wake of the devastating Covid-19 pandemic, and in order to stave off the potential for mass unemployment that may result, governments around the world have looked to deploy targeted work time reduction schemes. Just a single example, the German 'Kurzarbeit' programme gives a picture of the extraordinary topicality of such schemes. This enabled a temporary reduction of regular working hours in

response to substantial decreases in demand for
labour within a firm. During the crisis, the scheme
provided workers whose hours have been reduced
with a minimum of 60 per cent of their lost pay. The
IMF has described the policy as the 'the gold standard
of such programs' worldwide.[2]

However, while such schemes should be welcomed
as a short-term measure to ward off unemployment
and retain jobs, we should remain sceptical of its long-
term viability as a model for change. The historical
example of the Great Depression of the 1930s should
give us pause here. Then, working time reduction
schemes were implemented in the US in an attempt to
mitigate mass unemployment. As historian Benjamin
Hunnicutt has noted, the thirty-five-hour working time
reduction scheme enacted by the Roosevelt administration of the 1930s was simply a preventive economic
stopgap to stave off the threat of looming unemployment, ready for an increase once the economic crisis
had abated.[3] Industry leaders of the period were eager
to reassert 'normal' working hours as soon as possible – regarding the increase in leisure time during this
period as having the potential to undermine work's
status as the 'centre of life'.[4] As Hunnicutt writes,

While recognizing leisure as an ally to consumption, businessmen such as Ford and Cowdrick, as

well as the Hoover Committee, nevertheless reaf-
firmed their faith that work was, and should remain,
the center of life. Ford, for example, while praising
the economic significance of leisure, cautioned that
'of course, there is a humanitarian side of the
shorter day and the shorter week, but dwelling on
that subject is likely to get one in trouble, for then
leisure may be put before work rather than after
work-where it belongs.'[5]

Once the worst of the economic crisis had receded,
the thirty-five-hour week was quickly abandoned, and
within a two-year period, average working hours in
the US increased again to forty-five. As the Autonomy
think tank has identified in its research on this history,
there are other similar examples of such schemes,
implemented as an economic intervention to protect
jobs in times of crisis, being abandoned once normal
economic activity resumes. In the UK, the working
time reductions of 1847 were rescinded as soon as
conditions improved, and it wasn't until nearly thirty
years later that the legislation for a maximum ten-
hour day was finally secured.[6]

The important lesson from history is that there are
multiple actors and strategies that need to be mobi-
lised in order to achieve social change. There is no
silver bullet for the implementation of a sustainable

long-term reduction in working hours: the demand
must come from multiple directions.

Social movements:
working less can save the planet and our future
As this book has explored, the fight for free time is
also, fundamentally, a fight for environmental and
social justice. It is therefore vital that contemporary
social movements tap into and incorporate political
demands that speak to the virtues of working time
reduction across the board.

One contemporary social movement that addresses
climate injustice through direct action is Extinction
Rebellion (XR). Since the protests held in London in
November 2018, where XR blocked several of the
main routes across the River Thames in an attempt
to bring the capital to a halt, XR has deployed civil
disobedience tactics with the aim to not only shut
down major infrastructure and cause as much disruption as possible, but also actively court mass arrests
from the police.[7] While we don't intend to assess the
merits or pitfalls of XR's strategic form of direct
action,[8] it appears that one of the reasons for the
recent loss in public support for the campaign stems
from its inability to articulate a strategic vision
beyond what it is against. As the failings of Climate
Camp and Occupy demonstrate, it is not enough to

simply suspend the normal running of things. Political demands need to express forms of class struggle that engage with and stimulate not only people's sense of injustice, but also their sense of a better future – one that directly speaks to improving their day-to-day lives.

The demand for a shorter working week can therefore be a platform around which collective organising and strike action can coalesce. We saw this sort of galvanising effect in the events called the 'Long Friday' on 24 October 1975 in Iceland. On the first day of the UN decade for women, the women of Iceland collectively took the day off from both paid and unpaid work in order to demonstrate to the men of the island the economic and social injustice women faced in both the domestic and public workplace.[9] Ninety per cent of Iceland's women took part in the strike, with twenty rallies being held across the country (the largest being in Reykjavik, with 25,000 women in attendance – an incredible number for a population of just 220,000 people).

The political effects of this collective action were tangible and are still felt in the country today. A year after the event took place, Iceland passed the Gender Equality Act, outlawing sex discrimination in workplaces and schools.[10] In addition, Vigdis Finnbogadottir, one of the campaign's lead organisers, became the world's first democratically elected female head of state.[11]

Today, we are witnessing something similar to the Long Friday taking place on a global scale in the form of the upsurge of climate strike protests. Organising under the 'Fridays for Future' banner, this growing movement has witnessed children from all over the world taking to the streets on Fridays in order to highlight the climate crisis and the social injustice being caused by political inaction in tackling the causes of climate breakdown. Inspiration should be taken from the Long Friday strike and from the political momentum created by the Fridays for Future movement. By joining forces with school children all over the world, withdrawing collective paid and unpaid labour would demonstrate its instrumental value while publicly reclaiming a working day as time in which to fight for all forms of social justice.[12]

Part of winning the battle to work less will be in changing the *qualitative* feeling of what constitutes a working day. While the fact that a Saturday away from the toil of labour is normalised for many across the world, we need to recognise that this was not always the case, but was in fact a historical achievement. Even as recently as the start of the twentieth century, most working people didn't get the two-day weekend many of us now take for granted. Its normalisation occurred with the hard-fought battles won by trade unions and social movements, who campaigned and politicised the right for workers to have two consecutive days off each week.

Claiming Fridays as a non-working day could be for the twenty-first century what the two-day weekend was for the workers' movements of the twentieth. However, the fight today is no longer confined to the factory floor but must be taken across all social domains, challenging and reclaiming the labour carried out by women in their roles as unpaid workers in the family home, and the future world of our school children.

Trade unions: time to reactivate their histories
One common theme in this history for reduced working time is the invaluable role that trade unions have played. As Robert Skidelsky notes, major reductions in hours worked have coincided with periods of union strength.[13] Prior to 1919, the working week in the UK was between fifty and sixty hours. The campaign for a shorter working week in the twentieth century gained traction in the 1890s, and by 1910 over 1.1 million UK workers had a forty-eight-hour week.[14] With the outbreak of the First World War in 1914, unions relented, allowing the government to increase working hours in order to help the war effort. However, this was on the condition that a shorter

working week was nationally instituted immediately
afterwards. As the Trades Union Congress (TUC)
notes, 'In 1919, the very first international convention
on working conditions established the eight-hour
working day and the 48-hour week.'[15]

The increasing influence of trade unions and the
improved conditions that they won for their members
resulted in membership numbers swelling, reaching
8.3 million by 1920. While the rest of the industrial
world experienced similar working time reduction,
the UK was unique in the primacy of union action in
this. As a report from the Resolution Foundation
notes, the single largest reduction in average working
hours in 1919 was the result of extensive collective
bargaining agreements actioned through years of
trade union campaigning.[16] With the union movement
leading the cause for reduced working hours, employers and the government found it increasingly difficult
to increase working hours. The battle of George
Square in 1919 and the national strike of 1926 demon-
strated the power of organised labour and the
willingness of trade unions to fight for worker freedom inside and outside the workplace.

Since the 1980s, the number of trade union
members in the UK has been steadily declining. The
effects of Thatcher's neoliberal counter-revolution
against organised labour continues to be felt today. As

of 2016, only 16 per cent of the UK's private sector workers were covered by collective bargaining agreements.[17] The unrelenting weakening of trade union power through neoliberal reforms has played a key role in working time reduction slipping off trade unions' restricted agenda. A combination of anti-trade union laws and the most right-wing Conservative government of a generation appears at first glance not to be the most fertile ground for a renaissance in trade unionism. However, we are beginning to see evidence of green shoots. In 2019, workers who were members of a trade union rose by a net 91,000, representing a third consecutive year in which the number of union members has grown after years of decline.[18] The 2019 figures also revealed that membership had increased in both the public and private sectors, across England, Wales and Scotland.[19] Trade unions' key role in implementing and sustaining the furlough scheme has always reinforced to the public the vital role it can play in protecting jobs through times of economic downturn and crisis.

While Covid provides the opportunity for trade unions to grow and play a key role in protecting jobs and livelihoods in the short term, profound technological and environmental challenges to the way we work also require trade unions to have a long-term strategy. As Alice Martin and Annie Quick argue in

Unions Renewed,[20] the threats of climate change and automation require unions to shift from being on the back foot (for example, resisting job losses caused by automation) to being on the front, i.e., finding ways to shape the economic and social use of technology in ways that benefit workers.[21] Demanding a reduction in working hours for their members speaks to both technological and environmental threats while also reviving trade unions' proud history of winning the fight for free time.

The Communication Workers Union (CWU), for example, have recently taken up the baton. Representing over 134,000 postal workers, it has made the case for a gradual reduction in working hours from thirty-nine to thirty-five hours a week by 2021, while retaining the same pay for its members. They argue that it shouldn't be only shareholders benefiting from the productivity gains generated from the automation of many of its parcel-processing facilities. In Ireland, the trade union Forsa recently added its voice to a reduction of working time across the economy in the form of a four-day week without a loss in pay for workers. This is in part a response to 'productivity improvements arising from new technologies and improved work organisation'.[22]

Germany's second largest trade union, Verdi, recently began their collective bargaining process for public transportation workers. Part of the negotiations will include a campaign for a general reduction in working time to a thirty-five-hour week.[23]

It will therefore be vital for trade unions to form a joined-up international effort to campaign for free time in order to achieve a reduction of working time in the twenty-first century. As Martin and Quick emphasise, the demand for free time in the face of multiple crises represents, for trade unions, a pivot away from defending work to one that defends 'the freedom of workers from work with an increase in leisure time'.[24]

Political parties: building power and the offer of hope
At the 2019 Labour Party Conference, the then Shadow Chancellor John McDonnell announced the party's official policy of pursuing a transition to a thirty-two-hour working week over the course of a decade. Here, the embrace of policies like this revealed a strategic imperative from the Labour leadership to move beyond the 2017 manifesto. A shorter working week, alongside policies like a Green New Deal, was the result of what journalist George Eaton referred to as Corbynism 2.0: an economic and social programme that attempted to not only undo neoliberalism, but to create and communicate a new vision of socialism fit for the twenty-first century.[25]

However, with a heavy general election defeat later the same year, the radical economic and social programme outlined under Corbyn and McDonnell's leadership came under intense scrutiny. Although Labour's poor performance at the election was mainly attributed to its Brexit position and Corbyn's unpopularity as leader,[26] political commentators and labour activists turned on the perceived feasibility of delivering on its manifesto pledges. Its shorter working week policy, in combination with free universal broadband and a national care service, lacked any overarching framing, resulting in what was perceived by the electorate as a range of individually undeliverable election promises:

> But individually popular policies are worthless unless the public accepts the collective programme. In Labour's case, they did not believe the party had the capacity to deliver its cornucopia of promises. Indeed, as Labour added pledges such as a four-day week, free universal broadband and £58bn of compensation for WASPI women, they were bewildered by its seemingly bottomless generosity.[27]

The general election loss, combined with the standing down of Jeremy Corbyn and John McDonnell as leader and shadow chancellor respectively, represented a major blow to campaigners and activists hoping for a Labour government committed to a radical policy on working time. In addition, the recriminations from the general election and the results of a bitterly divided party, saw such policies being dismissed as strategically 'naive', 'unpopular' or the kind of economic 'luxury' that Labour should only pursue in times of economic strength. The temptation for a Labour Party 'under new management' in the future appears to be to move towards the centre ground and away from the more 'radical' elements of the previous manifesto.

But this narrative belies two important facts: firstly, that the greatest reductions in working time have occurred *not* in times of economic strength, but in the periods following two catastrophic world wars. To believe that we can only have improved living standards, including more free time, once 'the economy has picked up' is a trap too often walked into: we must contest this framing rather than accept it. There is an enormous amount of wealth in our economies, but it is incredibly badly distributed: only 12 per cent of households own around 50 per cent of private wealth (£7 trillion), and we are the ninth most unequal country when it comes to income in the OECD.[28]

Secondly, far from being buried with Corbynism, this policy remains popular, and there now appears

to be increasing political support across the progressive spectrum. Polling carried out in summer 2020
suggests that rather than a four-day working week
being perceived as too radical, the opposite is in fact
the case: working less is becoming common sense for
both workers and businesses alike. Sixty-three per
cent of the public supported the introduction of a
four-day working week, with only 12 per cent oppos-
ing it. In addition, 57 per cent of Conservative and 70
per cent of Labour voters were in favour.[29] When 515
business leaders were consulted over their support for
a four-day working week, 79 per cent answered that
they were either 'quite' or 'very open' to the idea,
with only 17 per cent responding negatively to the
idea.[30]

Both in the UK and internationally, calls for a
shorter working week have garnered support across
the whole spectrum of progressive parties. In response
to the pandemic, Scotland's First Minister Nicola
Sturgeon has advocated for businesses to allow
employees to work a four-day week without a loss in
pay, in recognition of the added care responsibilities
workers face during the pandemic.[31] Other prominent
liberal politicians such as New Zealand Prime
Minister Jacinda Ardern and Finland's Sanna Marin
have also expressed support for a four-day week under
the remit of enhancing flexible working and creating

the social conditions in which greater work–life balance can be achieved.[32]

As is to be expected, prominent socialist voices such as Bernie Sanders and Alexandria Ocasio-Cortez have also spoken in support of shorter working week policy programmes aimed at increasing workers' rights.[33] Turning to more concrete proposals, Spain's Deputy Prime Minister Pablo Iglesias announced that the coalition government would be exploring the possibility of shortening the working week to four days,[34] with the Spanish Ministry of Labour considering introducing a pilot subsidy scheme for companies wishing to pursue shorter working hours.[35]

While it's true that Labour struggled to encapsulate and communicate its manifesto in a way that was both effective and feasible, the uncompromising hostility the Left received from a supposedly 'progressive majority' in recent elections[36] reveals the blinkered and uncompromising position adopted by the political centre ground. The reality is that, even if Corbyn's Labour or a Democratic Party with Sanders as president had won their respective elections, they would have been in *government rather than in power*. As Jeremy Gilbert reminds us, no left-wing administration has ever implemented a successful reform programme without 'a large-scale movement of workers, citizens and activists that supported it, challenged its opponents in the media and was willing to stand up to economic blackmails from capitalists'.[37]

Even the most optimistic Corbyn or Sanders supporter would have to admit that the chances of implementing their respective policy agendas would have been extremely difficult due to the strength of capitalist forces built up after forty years of neoliberal hegemony. As Gilbert eloquently argues, 'it's not who is in government that matters; it's the overall balance of forces in society.'[38] It is therefore imperative that radical ideas such as a four-day week are incorporated into the project of building power in a mutually reinforcing manner: in the first instance, the demand provokes desire for what would be of huge benefit to working people, but this will in turn need to be reinforced by the backing of grassroots social movements and trade unions if it is to make headway. The goal, with this popular pressure in hand, is to force political parties of the Centre and the Left to consider working time reduction as a policy area that could garner support and be defended not only in an election, but over the course of a premiership.[39]

The fight for a shorter working week will therefore be just that: a fight. While the case for a radical policy agenda must be kept alive in political parties of the Left through members, activists, progressive think tanks and journalists, the fight for free time will be won by building power in the workplace and across society at large. As outlined above, the actors of this change will not only be trade unions but also social movements and those politicians acutely aware of the historical moment we find ourselves in. Together, by communicating and establishing a new narrative of the future based on sustainability, gender equality, human flourishing and, above all, *freedom*, these forces have the capacity to make the next big change to our working lives.

Notes

Introduction:
A Fight as Old as Capitalism Itself

1. The stonemasons in Australia were preceded marginally by Samuel Parnell in Aotearoa (New Zealand), a carpenter who won an eight-hour day from his employer in early 1840.

2. Sparrow, J. and Sparrow, J., *Radical Melbourne* (Carlton North, Victoria: Vulgar Press, 2001).

3. Ibid.

4. See: Kelly, J. 'Finland Prime Minister's Aspirational Goal of a Six-Hour, Four-Day Workweek: Will It Ever Happen?', *Forbes*, 2020. Available from: forbes.com/sites/jackkelly/2020/01/08/finlands-prime-ministers-aspirational-goal-of-a-six-hour-four-day-workweek-will-this-ever-happen. See also: Elliott, L., 'John McDonnell pledges shorter working week and no loss of pay', *The Guardian*, 2019. Available from: theguardian.com/politics/2019/sep/23/john-mcdonnell-pledges-shorter-working-week-and-no-loss-of-pay. For

Jacinda Adern see: Roy, E., 'Jacinda Ardern flags four-day working week as way to rebuild New Zealand after Covid-19', *The Guardian*, 2020. Available from: the guardian.com/world/2020/may/20/jacinda-ardern-flags-four-day-working-week-as-way-to-rebuild-new-zealand-after-covid-19.

5. Paul, K., 'Microsoft Japan tested a four-day work week and productivity jumped by 40 per cent', *The Guardian*, 2019. Available from: theguardian.com/technology/2019/nov/04/microsoft-japan-four-day-work-week-productivity.

6. Fox-Leonard, B., 'Fitter, happier, more productive: what it's really like to work for a company where no one does a five-day week', *The Telegraph*, 2020. Available from: telegraph.co.uk/family/life/fitter-happier-productive-really-like-work-company-no-one-does.

7. Gopal, P., *Insurgent Empire: Anticolonial Resistance and British Dissent* (London: Verso Books, 2019); Ramdin, R., *The Making of the Black Working Class in Britain* (London: Verso Books, 2017).

8. Kara, S., *Modern Slavery: A Global Perspective* (New York: Columbia University Press, 2017).

9. Piketty T., *Capital in the Twenty-First Century* (Harvard: Harvard University Press, 2014).

10. ONS, 'Total Wealth in Great Britain: April 2016 to March 2018', 2019. Available from: ons.gov.uk/people-populationandcommunity/personalandhousehold

finances/incomeandwealth/bulletins/totalwealthin-greatbritain/april2016tomarch2018.

11. Christophers, B., *Rentier Capitalism: Who Owns the Economy, and Who Pays for It?* (London: Verso, 2020); Standing, G., *The Corruption of Capitalism: Why Rentiers Thrive and Work Does Not Pay* (London: Biteback, 2017).

12. TUC, 'Workers in the UK put in more than £35 billion worth of unpaid overtime last year – TUC analysis', 2020. Available from: tuc.org.uk/news/workers-uk-put-more-ps35-billion-worth-unpaid-overtime-last-year-tuc-analysis.

13. TUC, 'Annual commuting time is up 21 hours compared to a decade ago, finds TUC', 2019. Available from: tuc.org.uk/news/annual-commuting-time-21-hours-compared-decade-ago-finds-tuc.

14. Cribb J. et al., 'Living standards, poverty and inequality in the UK', 2018. Institute for Fiscal Studies.

15. Hick R. and Lanau A., *In-work Poverty in the UK* (Cardiff: Cardiff University, 2017).

16. ONS, 'Contracts that do not guarantee a minimum number of hours: September 2017', 2017. Available from: ons.gov.uk/employmentandlabourmarket/people inwork/earningsandworkinghours/articles/contractst-hatdonotguaranteeaminimumnumberofhours/september2017.

17. BBC, 'Amazon to create 7,000 UK jobs', 2020. Available from: bbc.co.uk/news/business-54009484#:~:text=Online

per cent20retail per cent20giant per cent20Amazon per cent20has,workforce per cent20to per cent20more per cent-20than per cent2040 per cent2C000.

18. HSE, 'Work-related stress, anxiety or depression statistics in Great Britain', 2019. Available from: hse.gov.uk/ statistics/causdis/stress.pdf.

19. Fulton, L., *Worker Representation in Europe* (Labour Research Department and ETUI, 2013).

20. IER, *A Manifesto for Labour Law: Towards a Comprehensive Revision of Workers' Rights* (London: Institute of Employment Rights, 2016).

21. Ibid.

22. Alston, P., *Statement on Visit to the United Kingdom, by Professor Philip Alston, United Nations Special Rapporteur on extreme poverty and human rights*, 2018. Available from: ohchr.org/Documents/Issues/Poverty/EOM_ GB_16Nov2018.pdf, p. 1.

23. Ibid., p. 17.

24. Skidelsky, R., *How to Achieve Shorter Working Hours* (London: Progressive Economy Forum, 2019). Available from: progressiveeconomyforum.com/wp-content/ uploads/2019/08/PEF_Skidelsky_How_to_achieve_ shorter_working_hours.pdf.

25. Frayne, D., *The Work Cure: Critical Essays on Work and Wellness* (Monmouth: PCCS Books, 2019), p. 122.

26. Bregman, R., 'The solution to just about everything: Working less', *The Correspondent*, April 2016. Available

from: thecorrespondent.com/4373/the-solution-to-just-about-everything-working-less/168119985-db3d3c10.

01 *Living in the Work-Obsessed Society*

1. Reform Committee of the South Wales Miners, 'The Miners' Next Step', in Coates, K. and Topham, T. (eds) *Workers' Control* (London: Panther Books, 1970), pp. 23–4.

2. It might also help us understand the inner logic of capitalism itself.

3. Marx's theory is, by his own acknowledgement, a distillation of the basic coordinates and logics of a capitalist economy and labour market; it is not comprehensive of all exceptions. We acknowledge that a minority of firms actually recognise the needs and desires of employees for more free time and for life outside work generally speaking; nonetheless, the bottom line of profit (and productivity) persists in a structural capacity, despite the progressive instincts of some business owners.

4. Marx, K., *Capital: A Critique of Political Economy, Volume One*, trans. by Ben Fowkes (London: Penguin, 1990), p. 375.

5. Ibid., p. 381.

6. Suzman, J., *Work: A History of How We Spend Our Time* (London: Bloomsbury, 2020).

7. Patel, R. and Moore, J., *A History of the World in Seven Cheap Things: A Guide to Capitalism, Nature,*

and the Future of the Planet (London: Verso, 2020).

8. Ibid., p. 96; Applebaum, H. A., *The Concept of Work: Ancient, Medieval and Modern* (Albany: State University of New York Press, 1992); Komlosy, A., *Work: The Last 1,000 Years* (London: Verso, 2018).

9. Patel and Moore, *A History of the World*, p. 109.

10. The agricultural origin of capitalist economies is discussed in great depth by Brenner (in Aston, T. H. and Philpin, C. H. E. (eds), *The Brenner Debate: Agrarian Class Structure and Economic Development in Pre-Industrial Europe* (Cambridge: Cambridge University Press, 1985); and Meiksins Wood, E., *The Origins of Capitalism: A Longer View* (London: Verso, 2017).

11. Marx called this process 'primitive accumulation' (Marx, *Capital*). See the succinct chapter on 'cheap work' by Patel and Moore, *A History of the World*, for a summary of this and other intertwined processes.

12. See: Elsworthy, E., 'A quarter of British adults have no savings, study reveals', *The Independent*, 2018. Available from: independent.co.uk/news/uk/home-news/ british-adults-savings-none-quarter-debt-cost-living- emergencies-survey-results-a8265111.htm.

13. Anderson, E., *Private Government* (Princeton: Princeton University Press, 2017).

14. Peterson, J. S., *American Automobile Workers, 1900–1933* (Albany: State University of New York, 1987), pp. 57, 72.

15. Anderson, *Private Government*, p. 49.

16. See: Goodley, S. and Ashby, J., 'Revealed: how Sports Direct effectively pays below minimum wage', *The Guardian*, 2015. Available from: theguardian.com/business/2015/dec/09/how-sports-direct-effectively-pays-below-minimum-wage-pay.

17. See: Goodley, S., 'Mike Ashley running Sports Direct like "Victorian workhouse"', *The Guardian*, 2016. Available from: theguardian.com/business/2016/jul/22/mike-ashley-running-sports-direct-like-victorian-workhouse.

18. See: Sainato, M., '"I'm not a robot": Amazon workers condemn unsafe, grueling conditions at warehouse', *The Guardian*, 2020. Available from: theguardian.com/technology/2020/feb/05/amazon-workers-protest-unsafe-grueling-conditions-warehouse.

19. Felstead, A., Green, F., Gallie, D. and Henseke, G., *Work Intensity in Britain: First Findings from the Skills and Employment Survey 2017* (Cardiff: Cardiff University, 2018). Available from: cardiff.ac.uk/__data/assets/pdf_file/0009/1309455/4_Intensity_Minireport_Final.pdf.

20. Ibid: 'Both teachers and nurses have experienced dramatic increases in these consequences of work intensification. Nearly nine out of ten teachers report

being often or always exhausted after work, up from three quarters in 2006; for nurses, the jump between the 1990s and the present decade is from 25 percent to 73 percent. Nearly four in ten teachers can be classified as in a High Strain job – as compared with 17 percent for all workers.'

21. HSE, 'Work-related stress, anxiety or depression statistics in Great Britain, 2020', 2020. Available from: hse.gov.uk/statistics/causdis/stress.pdf.

22. Murray, N., *Burnout Britain: Overwork in an Age of Unemploymy* (London: Autonomy, Compass and the 4 Day Week Campaign, 2020). Available from: autonomy.work/wp-content/uploads/2020/10/4DW-mentalhealth_cumpass_4dwcORANGE_C-v2.pdf.

23. Morris, N., 'We're working an extra "28 hours per month" in lockdown', *Metro*, 2020. Available from: metro.co.uk/2020/05/05/working-extra-28-hours-per-month-lockdown-12654962.

02 *Untapped Potential: Labour-Saving Technology and Human Flourishing*

1. Williams, R. *Towards 2000* (London: Penguin, 1985), pp. 91–2.

2. Keynes, J. M., *The Collected Writings of John Maynard Keynes. Volume X: Essays in Biography* (first published 1933), ed. by Robinson, A. and Moggridge, D. (Cambridge: Cambridge University Press, 2013).

3. ILO, *Working Time Around the World* (London: Routledge, 2007).

4. 'Our superiority complex, Keynes mused, is perhaps
insatiable'. Keynes, J. M., *The Collected Writings of
John Maynard Keynes. Volume X: Essays in Biography*
(2013, first published 1933). In: Robinson, A. and
Moggridge, D. (eds). (Cambridge: Cambridge University Press, 2013).

5. Ibid., p. 366.

6. Ibid., p. 445.

7. Crespo, R., *Philosophy of the Economy: an Aristotelian Approach* (New York: Springer, 2013), p. 105.

8. Skidelsky, R. *How to Achieve Shorter Working Hours*
(London: Progressive Economy Forum, 2019). Available from: progressiveeconomyforum.com/wp-content/
uploads/2019/08/PEF_Skidelsky_How_to_achieve_
shorter_working_hours.pdf.

9. Bolt, J., Timmer, M. and Luiten van Zanden, J., 'GDP
per capita since 1820', in Luiten van Zanden, J. et al.
(eds) *How Was Life? Global Well-being Since 1820*
(OECD Publishing, 2014), dx.doi.org/10.1787/97892
64214262-7-en.

10. See: Jones, J., 'What Can 19th Century Labour Activists Teach Us About Transforming Work After Covid?',
Autonomy, 2020. Available from: autonomy.work/
portfolio/19thcenturyworkingtime.

11. Scott, P. and Spadavecchia, A. 'Did the 48-hour week

damage Britain's industrial competitiveness?', *Economic History Society* 64: 4, 2011, 1266–88.

12. Jones, 'What Can 19th Century Labour Activists Teach Us?'; Hutchins, B. L. and Harrison, A., *A History of Factory Legislation* (London: P. S. King & Son, 1911).

13. Bangham, G., *The Times They Aren't a-Changin'* (London: Resolution Foundation, 2020). Available from: resolutionfoundation.org/app/uploads/2020/01/The-times-they-arent-a-changin.pdf.

14. Gorz, A., *Capitalism, Socialism, Ecology* (London: Verso, 1994), p. 45.

15. Marcuse, H., *Eros and Civilization: A Philosophical Enquiry into Freud* (London: Abacus, 1973), p. 152.

16. Ibid., p. 156.

17. Marcuse's argument prefigures more recent calls for 'full automation' or 'luxury communism'. See Srnicek, N. and Williams, A., *Inventing the Future: Postcapitalism and a World Without Work* (London: Verso, 2015); and Bastani, A., *Fully Automated Luxury Communism: A Manifesto* (London: Verso, 2019).

18. See Benanav, A. *Automation and the Future of Work* (London: Verso, 2020); and Smith, J. *Smart Machines and Service Work: Automation in an Age of Stagnation* (London: Reaktion Books, 2020).

19. West, E.G., 'Adam Smith's Two Views on the Division of Labour', *Economica* 31: 121, 1964, 23–32.

20. Smith, A., *An Inquiry into the Nature and Causes of*

the Wealth of the Nations (Indianapolis: Liberty Classics, volume 2, 1976), pp. 781–2.

21. Russell, B., *Roads to Freedom* (Nottingham: Spokesman Books, 2006), p. 88.

22. Ibid., p. 89.

23. Bataille, G., *The Accursed Share, Volume I*, trans. by R. Hurley (London: Zone Books, 1988); Bataille, G., *The Accursed Share, Volumes II and III*, trans. by R. Hurley (London: Zone Books, 1992).

24. Weeks, K., *The Problem with Work: Feminism, Marxism, AntiWork Politics, and Post-Work Imaginaries* (Durham: Duke University Press, 2011), p. 86.

25. Ibid., p. 83.

26. Workplace pressure from management is usually mentioned in the same breath as 'Taylorism', indexing the 'scientific management' studies of Frederick Taylor in the early twentieth century. Taylor's primary thesis – that in order to get the most out of your staff, one must control their time and even their bodily motions as precisely as possible – forms the basis of the majority of subsequent management strategies across the world. Harry Braverman goes as far as to call Taylorism 'the verbalisation of the capitalist mode of production'. Braverman, H., *Labour and Monopoly Capital. The Degradation of Work in the Twentieth Century* (New York: Monthly Review Press, 1974), p. 60.

27. Lenin, V. I., 'A Scientific System of Sweating', in *Collected Works*, Vol. 18 (London: Lawrence and Wishart, 1963), pp. 594–5.

28. Lenin, V. I., 'The Urgent Problems of the Soviet Rule: Higher Productivity of Labor', in *Collected Works*, Vol. 27 (Moscow: Progress Publishers, 1965; originally published in 1918), p. xxii.

29. Lenin, V. I., *Selected Works* (New York, NY: International Publishers, 1971; originally published 1918), p. 417.

30. Postone, M., *Time, Labour, and Social Domination* (Cambridge: Cambridge University Press, 1991).

31. Dyer-Witheford, N., *Cyber-Marx: Struggles and Circuits of Struggle in High-Technology Capitalism* (Chicago: University of Illinois Press, 1999), p. 9.

32. Weeks, *The Problem with Work*, p. 84. Similar properties can be found in advocates of a 'Green New Deal'. See Chapter 4.

33. The question, in many ways, is whether industrialism should outlast capitalism. For authors such as Postone, this is impossible: the two are inseparable. See Postone, *Time*.

34. Weeks, *The Problem with Work*, p. 86.

35. Ibid., p. 87.

36. This is in obvious opposition to the Aristotelian ethics that motivated Keynes's common sense that work is merely a means towards the good life, for example.

The 'work dogma' is a concept pursued further by David Frayne. Frayne, D., *The Refusal of Work* (London: Zed Books, 2015).

37. Weeks, *The Problem with Work*, p. 87.

38. Weeks, *The Problem with Work*, p. 107.

39. See, for example, Postone, *Time*, as well as much of Andre Gorz's work, for example: Gorz, A., *Farewell to the Working Class* (London: Pluto, 1982).

40. We discuss strategy further in Chapter 5.

41. Chapman, B., 'Majority of UK workers support four-day working week, study finds', *The Independent*, 2019. Available from: independent.co.uk/news/business/news/four-day-working-week-pay-transparency-yougov-poll-a8941891.html; Smith, M., 'Eurotrack: Europeans support introducing a four day working week', YouGov, 2019. Available from: yougov.co.uk/topics/economy/articles-reports/2019/03/15/eurotrack-europeans-support-introducing-four-day-w.

42. TUC, 'A future that works for working people', 2018. Available from: tuc.org.uk/research-analysis/reports/future-works-working-people.

03 *Women's Time and the Shorter Working Week*

1. Federici, S., *Revolution at Point Zero: Housework, Reproduction, and Feminist Struggle* (New York: Autonomedia, 2012 [1975]), p. 22.

2. For useful resources on this topic, see: Trafford, J., 'Race and Work' factsheet, Autonomy, 2018. Available from: autonomy.work/wp-content/uploads/2018/11/Race-and-Work-V4-3.pdf; Gebrial, D. 'Dangerous Brown Workers: How Race and Migration Politics Shape the Platform Labour Market', in Muldoon, J. and Stronge, W. (eds) *Platforming Equality* (Hampshire: Autonomy, 2020). Available from: autonomy.work/portfolio/platformingequality.

3. Hester defines reproductive labour as 'the activities that nurture future workers, regenerate the current work force, and maintain those who cannot work – that is, the set of tasks that together maintain and reproduce life, both daily and generationally'. Hester, H., 'Care Under Capitalism: The Crisis of "Women's Work"', *IPPR* 24: 4, 2018, 343–52.

4. There is a kind of mirror image version of the work ethic at play in the domestic sphere, with the studious housewife as its ideal subject. See Weeks. K., *The Problem with Work: Feminism, Marxism, Anti-Work Politics and Post-Work Imaginaries* (Durham: Duke University Press, 2011).

5. Fraser, N., 'Charting Shifts and Moving Forward in Abnormal Times: An Interview with Nancy Fraser',

An International Journal for Moral Philosophy 15: 1, 2016, 31.

6. Hall. C., 'The History of the Housewife', in Malos, E. (ed.) *The Politics of Housework* (London: Allison & Busby, 1980).

7. Seabrook, J., 'In and Out of Work: an interview with Jeremy Seabrook', Autonomy, 2018. Available from: autonomy.work/wp-content/uploads/2018/08/Jeremy-Seabrook-interview-V3.pdf.

8. Ibid., p. 61.

9. Pettinger, L., *What's Wrong with Work?* (Bristol: Policy Press, 2019), p. 56.

10. Ibid.

11. There is no need to dwell on arguments that there is something 'natural' or 'essential' about women that makes them better suited to housework. In Dalla Costa and James's words: 'a woman doesn't get more or less exhausted than a man from washing and cleaning.' Dalla Costa, M. and James, S. 'Women and the Subversion of the Community', in Malos, *The Politics of Housework.*

12. Pettinger, *What's Wrong with Work?*, p. 56.

13. The World Bank, 'The World Bank in Gender', 2020. Available from: worldbank.org/en/topic/gender/overview. In the US in 1970, 32 million American women were understood to be in the labour market; by 1990, the number was 57 million; and in 2009, 72 million.

Bureau for Labor Statistics, 'Women in the Labor Force, 1970–2009'. Available from: bls.gov.

14. ONS, 'Annual Population Survey – Employment by occupation by sex', 2020. Available from: nomisweb. co.uk/datasets/aps168/reports/employment-by-occupation?compare=K02000001; see also Khurana, I. and Kikuchi, L., 'Jobs at Risk Index (JARI)', Autonomy, 2020. Available from: autonomy.work/portfolio/jari.

15. The poverty line is usually understood, at least in the Global North, as two-thirds the median average pay of the country in question. For a visualisation of this data, see: Khurana and Kikuchi, 'Jobs at Risk Index'.

16. Arenofsky, J., *Work–Life Balance* (Santa-Barbara: Greenwood, 2017), p. 4.

17. Martin, A. and Scurrah, E., *Reclaiming Women's Time: Achieving Gender Equality in a World with Less Work* (London: New Economics Foundation, 2021).

18. Wood, W., *Despotism on Demand* (Cornell: Cornell University Press, 2020); Cant, C. *Riding for Deliveroo* (London: Polity, 2018). Taylor, 2017, p. 42.

19. Women's Budget Group, 'Women, Employment and Earnings', 2018. Available from: wbg.org.uk/wp-content/uploads/2018/10/Employment-November-2018-w-cover.pdf.

20. Skills for Care, 'The state of the adult social care sector and workforce in England', 2019. Available from: skillsforcare.org.uk/adult-social-care-workforce-data/

Workforce-intelligence/documents/State-of-the-adult-social-care-sector/State-of-Report-2019.pdf.

21. Hester, 'Care Under Capitalism', pp. 343–52.

22. Hester, H. and Srnicek, N., 'The Crisis of Social Repro-duction and the End of Work', Open Mind, 2018. Available from: bbvaopenmind.com/wp-content/uploads/2018/03/BBVA-OpenMind-Helen-Hester-Nick-Srnicek-The-Crisis-of-Social-Reproduction-and-the-End-of-Work.pdf. See also: Hester, H. and Srnicek, N., *After Work* (London: Verso, 2020).

23. Hester and Srnicek, 'The Crisis of Social Reproduction'.

24. The over-sixty-five population in the UK is set to increase from 11.6 million today to 15.4 million by 2030, and over 20 million by 2050. The 'oldest olds' (over-eighty-fives) are set to double from 1.6 million today to 3.2 million by 2041 and 5.1 million by 2066, equalling 7 per cent of the population. Age UK, 'Later Life UK Factsheet', Available from: ageuk.org.uk/global assets/age-uk/documents/reports-and-publications/later_life_uk_factsheet.pdf.

25. See Sheryl Sandberg's *Lean In* (New York: Alfred A Knopf, 2013). For a critique of this position, see Nicole Ashcroft's *New Prophets of Capital* (London: Verso/Jacobin, 2015).

26. ONS, 'Women shoulder the responsibility of "unpaid work"', 2016. Available from: visual.ons.gov.uk/the-value-of-your-unpaid-work.

27. Ibid.

28. Arlie Hochschild coined the term 'the second shift' in her 1989 book entitled *The Second Shift: Working Parents and the Revolution at Home*. Duncombe and Marsden identify the 'triple shift' of women as constituting the burden of paid employment, domestic labour and tending to the emotional care of family members and loved ones: 'Women's "Triple Shift" (Gender and Emotional Work in Families)', *Sociology Review* 4: 4, 1995, 30.

29. Hargreaves, D., 'Women at work designing a company fit for the future', Friends Provident, 2019. Available from: friendsprovidentfoundation.org/wp-content/uploads/2019/06/Women-at-work-Download.pdf, p. 5.

30. Weeks, *The Problem with Work*, p. 163.

31. Murray, *Burnout Britain*, p. 5.

32. Ibid.

33. Wages Against Housework pamphlet contained within Federici's later work , *Revolution at Point Zero*.

34. Ibid., p. 16.

35. Ibid., p. 18.

36. Reid, M., *The Economics of Household Production* (New York: John Riley, 1934).

37. Gershuny, O. and Sullivan, O., *What We Really Do All Day: Insights from the Centre for Time Use Research* (London: Penguin, 2019).

38. Ibid., p. 143.

39. The ONS offered an estimate in 2018 of the total value of unpaid work *including* intermediary goods, raw materials and so on of £1.24 trillion, or 63.1 per cent per cent of national GDP (larger in size than the UK's non-financial corporation sector). ONS, 'Household satellite account, UK: 2015 ad 2016', 2018. Available from: ons.gov.uk/economy/nationalaccounts/satellite-accounts/articles/householdsatelliteaccounts/2015and2016estimates.

40. Such accounting is a political tool. In Federici's words: 'In this respect nothing can be more effective than to show that our female virtues have already a calculable money value: until today only for capital, increased in the measure that we were defeated, from now on, against capital, for us, in the measure that we organize our power' (*Revolution at Point Zero*, p. 20).

41. Ibid.

42. Harper, A. and Stronge, W. (eds) *The Shorter Working Week: A Radical and Pragmatic Proposal* (Hampshire: Autonomy, 2019). Available from: autonomy.work/portfolio/the-shorter-working-week-a-report-from-autonomy-in-collaboration-with-members-of-the-4-day-week-campaign.

43. According to a 2016 OECD report, the seven countries with the highest share of male parental users (Iceland, Sweden, Portugal, Norway, Luxembourg, Belgium, and Germany), all have father-specific entitlements to

paid parental leave. OECD, *Background Brief on Fathers' Leave and Its Use*, March 2016. Available from: oecd.org/backgrounder-fathers-use-of-leave.pdf.

44. See Dolores Hayden's *The Grand Domestic Revolution* (1982) for an in-depth analysis of the material feminist movement in nineteenth century America.

45. For examples of long-term care centres, see Farruggia, F. et al., *Long Term Care Centres: Making Space for Ageing* (Hampshire: Autonomy, 2020). Available from: autonomy.work/wp-content/uploads/2020/11/LTCCv7.pdf. For examples of community open work-spaces, see Farruggia, F. et al. *The New Normal: A Blueprint for Remote Working* (Hampshire: Autonomy, 2020). Available from: autonomy.work/2020_OCT26_RWB.pdf.

04 *Time for the Environment*

1. Soper, K., *Post-Growth Living: For an Alternative Hedonism* (London: Verso, 2020), p. 185.

2. The urgency of action on climate was starkly under-lined by the Intergovernmental Panel on Climate Change (IPCC) 'Emissions Gap' report from 2019. It concluded that nations must reduce emissions by 7.6 per cent per year from 2020 to 2030 to achieve the goal of keeping temperature rises to a maximum of 1.5°C and 2.7 per cent per year for the 2°C goal (IPCC, 2019). Reducing carbon emissions is

of course not the only environmental challenge facing us.

3. We note that there are sometimes distinctions between 'degrowth' and 'post-growth' positions – the former generally representing a perspective geared at actively contracting economic activity, while the latter might be characterised as being 'agnostic' about growth and intent on shifting focus to other metrics of prosperity.

4. D'Alisa, G., Demaria, F., Kallis, G., *Degrowth: A Vocabulary for a New Era* (New York: Routledge, 2015), p. 3.

5. Corlet Walker, C., ' "Green growth" is not the solution', CUSP, 2019. Available from: cusp.ac.uk/themes/aetw/blog-ccw-decoupling-debunked.

6. Philipps, L., 'The Degrowth Delusion', *openDemocracy*, 2019. Available from: opendemocracy.net/en/oureconomy/degrowth-delusion.

7. See Gorz, A., *Capitalism, Socialism, Ecology* (London: Verso, 2012), p. 33.

8. Schneider, F., Kallis, G. and Martinez-Alier, J. 'Crisis or Opportunity? Economic Degrowth for Social Equity and Ecological Sustainability. Introduction to This Special Issue', *Journal of Cleaner Production* 18: 6, 2010, 511–18.

9. Ibid., p. 513.

10. The 'circular economy' is a term used not only by environmental campaigners but also by various

corporations intending, most likely, to greenwash their operations. In some circumstances, the circular economy is said to promise huge growth in particular sectors. However, if a circular economic model was carried out thoroughly – that is, following maximum reuse, maximum longevity and maximum recyclability principles – it is hard to imagine a scenario of growth anywhere near what we have known until now. For an introduction to this tension between different uses and abuses of the 'circular' label, see Will Jamieson's blog: 'Unfurling the circular economy: separating substance from style', Autonomy, 2020. Available from: autonomy.work/portfolio/circulareconomy.

11. A. Hayden, *Sharing the Work, Sparing the Planet – Work Time, Consumption and Ecology* (London: Zed Books, 1999).

12. Schor, J., *The Overworked American* (New York: Basic Books, 1992).

13. In an earlier study of similar scale, Knight et al. had investigated the effect of working hours against three environmental indicators: ecological footprint, carbon footprint and carbon dioxide emissions.. The study concluded that working time in high-income countries is significantly associated with environmental pressures (i.e., all environmental indicators stated above) and thus a reduction in working hours at a macro level 'may be an attractive target for policies promoting

environmental sustainability', p. 698, Knight, K. W., Rosa, E. A. and Schor, J. B., 'Could Working Hours Reduce Pressures on the Environment? a Cross-National Panel Analysis of OECD Countries, 1970–2007', *Global Environmental Change* 23: 4, 2013, 691–700.

14. Fremstad, A., Paul, M. and Underwood, A., 'Work Hours and CO_2 Emissions: Evidence from U.S. Households', *Review of Political Economy* 31: 1, 2 January 2019, 42–59, doi.org/10.1080/09538259.2019.1592950.

15. Whether this decoupling is indeed possible is a point of contemporary debate. See Christie, I., Gallant, B. and Mair, S., 'Growing pain: the delusion of boudless economic growth' (CUSP 2019). Available from: cusp. ac.uk/themes/aetw/blog-growth-delusion.

16. Pollin, R., 'De-Growth vs a Green New Deal', *New Left Review* 112, July–August 2018.

17. Frankel, B., *Fictions of Sustainability: The Politics of Growth and Post-Capitalist Futures* (Melbourne: Greenmeadows, 2018).

18. For instance, congresswoman Alexandria Ocasio-Cortez presented a resolution to the House of Representatives that proposed a Green New Deal for the US, to include – in its compressive plan of economic reform – a jobs guarantee for every US citizen (Ocasio-Cortez, A., 'Resolution Recognizing the Duty of the Federal Government to Create a Green New Deal', Resolution presented to the House of Representatives,

2018. Available from: ocasio-cortez.house.gov/sites/
ocasio-cortez.house.gov/files/Resolution per cent20on
per cent20a per cent20Green per cent20New per cent-
20Deal.pdf. In the UK, the Labour Party's 2019
manifesto proposed a version of the Green New Deal
under the remit of 'A Green Industrial Revolution'.
The economist Yanis Varoufakis went one step further
in articulating an international Green New Deal that
aims to create environmental and social justice under
the categories of production, innovation and repara-
tion. See Varoufakis, Y. and Adler, D., 'It's time for
nations to unite around an International Green
New Deal', *The Guardian,* 2019) Available from:
theguardian.com/commentisfree/2019/apr/23/interna-
tional-green-new-deal-climate-change-global-
response.

19. Friedman, T., 'A Warning from the Garden', *The New
York Times*, 2007. Available from: nytimes.com/2007/
01/19/opinion/19friedman.html.

20. Pettifor, A., *The Case for the Green New Deal* (London:
Verso, 2019).

21. Elliott, L. et al., *A Green New Deal: Joined-up Policies
to Solve the Triple Crunch of the Credit Crisis, Climate
Change and High Oil Prices.* (London: New Economics Foundation, 2008). Available from: neweconomics.
org/uploads/files/8f737ea195fe56db2f_xbm6ihwb1.
pdf.

22. Ibid., p. 1.

23. Pettifor, *The Case for the Green New Deal*, p. 7.

24. In our view, the GND can stray too close to the ideology and variety of capitalism from which it has been cast – that is to say: industrialism.

25. Duncombe and Marsden, 'Women's "Triple Shift"', p. 30.

26. Harper and Stronge, *The Shorter Working Week*.

27. The jobs guarantee has also been picked up across the Atlantic in the UK, both as part of the Labour Party's 'Green New Deal' and as a proposal for Covid recovery (TUC, 'Workers in the UK').

28. Aronoff, K., Battistoni, A., Aldana Cohen, D. and Riofrancos, T., *A Planet to Win: Why We Need a Green New Deal* (London: Verso, 2019), p. 88.

29. Ocasio-Cortez, 'Recognizing the Duty of the Federal Government'.

30. Pettifor, A., *The Case for the Green New Deal* (London: Verso, 2019), p. 99.

31. Ibid.

32. Ibid., p. 100.

33. Peck, J., *Workfare States* (New York: Guildford Press, 2001).

34. For other criticisms of a jobs guarantee, see Standing, G., 'Why a Job Guarantee is a bad joke for the precariat – and for freedom', openDemocracy, 2018. Available from: neweconomics.opendemocracy.net.

And Sligar, D. and Sturgess, H., 'Would a job guarantee be Work for the Dole 2.0?', Inside Story, 2020. Available from: insidestory.org.au.

35. Lele, S., 'Environment and Well-Being: A Perspective from the Global South', *New Left Review* 123, May–June 2020.

36. Ibid., pp. 42–5.

37. Jackson, T., and Victor, P., 'Productivity and Work in the "Green Economy": Some Theoretical Reflections and Empirical Tests', *Environmental Innovation and Societal Transitions* 1: 1, 2011, 101–8, doi.org/10.1016/j.eist.2011.04.005.

38. Aronoff et al., *A Planet to Win*. In their arguments for a GND, these authors also draw on the original New Deal, as we have here.

39. Ibid., p. 7.

40. Ibid., p. 91.

41. Ibid., p. 89.

42. Kate Soper's work on consumerism and its discontents touches on similar themes. See Soper, K, 'Alternative Hedonism, Culture Theory and the Role of Aesthetic Revisioning', *Cultural Studies*, 22: 5, 2008, 567–7; and 'The interaction of policy and experience: an "alternative hedonist" optic', in: M. Koch and O. Mont, eds. *Sustainability and the Political Economy of Welfare* (London: Routledge, 2016) pp. 186–200. In her recent book *Post-Growth Living: For an Alternative Hedonism*

(London: Verso, 2020), she makes the case for an 'alternative hedonism' that channels the widespread desire to break with our addiction to electronic gadgetry, 'fast fashion' and unhealthy consumption habits.

43. Aronoff et al., *A Planet to Win*, p. 92.

05 *The Struggle for the Shorter Working Week?*

1. Bookchin, M., *The Ghost of Anarcho-Syndicalism* (1992). Available from: dwardmac.pitzer.edu/anarchist_archives/bookchin/ghost2.html.

2. IMF, 'Kurzarbeit: Germany's Short-Time Work Benefit', 2020. Available from: imf.org/en/News/Articles/2020/06/11/na061120-kurzarbeit-germanys-short-time-work-benefit.

3. Hunnicutt, B., *Work Without End: Abandoning Shorter Hours for the Right to Work* (Philadelphia: Temple University Press, 1988).

4. There are evident similarities with the UK government's Covid-19 furlough scheme and other introduced measures. In April 2020, Conservative minister Iain Duncan Smith argued against the introduction of a universal basic income, as it would be a 'disincentive to work'. This response is representative of a shared fear among MPs that the experience of new welfare measures and working practices would change public opinion; getting back to 'normal' after Covid became an imperative as soon as possible, and even against the

well-known health considerations involved. See 'Coronavirus: Iain Duncan Smith says don't bring in universal basic income during pandemic as it would be 'disincentive to work'', *Independent*, 2020. Available from: independent.co.uk/news/uk/politics/coronavirus-uk-update-universal-basic-income-iain-duncan-smith-a9411251.html.

5. Hunnicut, *Work Without End*, p. 46.

6. Jones, 'What Can 19th Century Labour Activists Teach Us?'.

7. In an interview with *The Guardian*, Roger Hallam, one of XR's founders, outlines the logic of the strategic approach taken regarding mass arrests: 'only through disruption, the breaking of laws, do you get the attention you need . . . only through sacrifice – the willingness to be arrested and go to prison – do people take seriously what you are saying. And . . . only through being respectful to ourselves, the public and the police, do we change the hearts and minds of our opponents'. Available from: theguardian.com/commentisfree/2019/may/01/extinction-rebellion-non-violent-civil-disobedience.

8. For direct critiques of XR's strategic approach, see James Butler's 'The Climate Crisis Deserves More Than Blocking Roads, Extinction Rebellion', *The Guardian*, 2018. Available from: theguardian.com/commentisfree/2018/nov/26/climate-crisis-blocking-

roads-extinction-rebellion-labour; and an 'Out of the Woods' blog post entitled: 'Extinction Rebellion: Not the Struggle We Need Part. 1', 2019. Available from: libcom.org.

9. Today, similar initiatives exist, for example the Women's Strike collective: womenstrike.org.uk.

10. Perez, C., *Invisible Women: Exposing Data Bias in a World Designed for Men* (London: Chatto & Windus, 2019), p. 69.

11. Ibid., p. 70.

12. Frey, P. and Schneider, C., *The Shorter Working Week: A Powerful Tool to Drastically Reduce Carbon Emissions* (Hampshire: Autonomy, 2019). Available from: autonomy.work.

13. Skidelsky, R., *How to Achieve Shorter Working Hours* (London: Progressive Economy Forum, 2019). Available from: progressiveeconomyforum.com/wp-content/uploads/2019/08/PEF_Skidelsky_How_to_achieve_shorter_working_hours.pdf.

14. Scott, P. and Spadavecchia, A., 'Did the 48-Hour Week Damage Britain's Industrial Competitiveness?', *Economic History Society* 64: 4, 2011, 1266–88, at 1269.

15. TUC, 'The TUC Workplace Manual 2016', 2016. Available from: tuc.org.uk/resource/tuc-workplace-manual-2016, p. 1.

16. Bangham, G., *The Times They Aren't a- Changin'*, p. 3.

17. ETUI, 2016, cited in Skidelsky, R., *How to Achieve Shorter Working Hours*, p. 22.

18. National Statistics, 'Trade Union Membership, UK 1995–2019: Statistical Bulletin', 2019. Available from: assets.publishing.service.gov.uk, p. 5.

19. Ibid., p. 18.

20. Martin, A. and Quick, A., *Unions Renewed: Building Power in an Age of Finance* (Cambridge: Polity Press, 2020).

21. Ibid., p. 130.

22. Callinan, K., 'General Secretary, Fórsa 4-Day Week Ireland Launch Thursday 26th September 2019', Fórsa, 2019. Available from: forsa.ie.

23. Harper, A., 'Achieving a Shorter Working Week Across Europe, Newsletter of the European Network for the Fair Sharing of Working Time', New Economics Foundation, 2020. Available from: neweconomics.org/uploads/files/workingtime-newsletter5.pdf.

24. Martin and Quick, *Unions Renewed*, p. 131.

25. Eaton, G., 'Corbynism 2.0: the radical ideas shaping Labour's future', *New Statesman*, 2018. Available from: newstatesman.com/politics/uk/2018/09/corbynism-20-radical-ideas-shaping-labour-s-future.

26. See Paul Mason's 'The Left, The Party & The Class: An Essay on the Future of the Labour Left' for a detailed breakdown of the general election defeat and the how Brexit and Corbyn's unpopularity as leader contributed

to it. Available from: medium.com/@paulmasonnews/
the-left-the-party-and-the-class-1ca7b6a959e6.

27. Eaton, G., 'Why Labour lost – and how it can recover
from an epic defeat', *New Statesman*, 2019. Available from:
newstatesman.com/politics/uk/2019/12/why-labour-
lost-and-how-it-can-recover-epic-defeat.

28. ONS, 'Total Wealth in Great Britain'; OECD, 'Income
Inequality', 2020. Available from: data.oecd.org/
inequality/ income-inequality.htm.

29. Survation, 'UK polling: 63 per cent support government exploring the idea of a four-day week', Autonomy,
2020. Available from: autonomy.work/portfolio/4day
weekpolling.

30. Survation, 'Polling of UK business leaders: 79 per cent
are supportive of a four-day working week', Autonomy, 2020. Available from: autonomy.work/portfolio/
business4daypolling.

31. Andrews, K., 'Coronavirus in Scotland: Nicola Sturgeon calls for four-day week as she eases lockdown',
The Times, 2020. Available from: thetimes.co.uk/
article/coronavirus-in-scotland-nicola-sturgeon-
calls-for-four-day-week-as-she-eases-lockdown-
782cbnl6k.

32. Media reports on Ardern and Marin advocating a four-
day week can be found at, respectively: theguardian.
com/world/2020/may/20/jacinda-ardern-flags-four-
day-working-week-as-way-to-rebuild-new-zealand-

after-covid-19 and lbc.co.uk/news/finlands-prime-min ister-sanna-marin-proposes-four.

33. Sanders's openness to cutting working hours can be found in the following news report: businessinsider. com/4-day-workweek-for-americans-bernie-sanders-2020-campaign-2019. In an Instagram post to her followers, Alexandria Ocasio-Cortez discussed the benefits of a four-day week and Keynes's prediction regarding a fifteen-hour work in the year 2030 (unfor- tunately she gets his name wrong). The video can be found at: youtube.com/watch?v=76ULzCyzCqs.

34. Orihuela, R., 'Spain's Government Is Studying a Four-Day Work Week', *Bloomberg*, 2020. Available from: bloomberg.com/news/articles/2020-12-03/spain-government-studying-4-day-work-week-deputy-pm-tells-rtve.

35. Stone, J., 'Spain's left-wing government could help companies switch to four-day working week', *The Independent*, 2020. Available from: independent. co.uk/news/uk/politics/four-day-week-spain-valencia-autonomy-b1761163.html.

36. Jo Swinson, the Liberal Democrats leader at the time of the election, refused to countenance any formal pact with Labour at the 2019 general election with Corbyn as leader. See Mason, R., 'Jo Swinson rules out Lib Dem pact with Labour under Jeremy Corbyn', *The Guardian*, 2019. Available from: theguardian.com/politics/2019/

jul/23/jo-swinson-rules-out-lib-dem-pact-with-labour-under-jeremy-corbyn. The Green Party also stood candidates in seats they had very little chance of winning, knowing that it would more than likely result in Labour losing their seat and handing it to the Conservatives. See Boobyer, L., 'Political rivals boo and shout "shame" at Green Party candidate Molly Scott Cato during speech', *GloucestershireLive*, 2019. Available from: gloucestershirelive.co.uk/news/gloucester-news/political-rivals-boo-shout-shame-3640317.

37. Gilbert, J., *Twenty-First Century Socialism* (Cambridge: Polity Press, 2020), p. 85.

38. Ibid.

39. In this sense, one of Corbynism's successes (in its failure) was to put working time reduction on the mainstream agenda (and into a manifesto) for the first time in generations. This could be the starting gun, rather than the funeral, for the political importance of the issue.